The Fitness Entrepreneur

**Strategies to open or grow a successful
mobile fitness business**

Robert Raymond   Derrick Wilburn

ISBN: 978-1-4276-5008-5

What fitness professionals are saying about "The Fitness Entrepreneur"

"The reason I love working as a mobile fitness professional is because it allows me to set my own hours and earn more money per session with little to no overhead. I am making more working less hours then most of the friends I have who are trainers and working in the gyms."

Brian Baird, Personal Trainer
Littleton Colorado

"I have worked as a mobile fitness personal trainer for over 15 years in the new York and new jersey area. It has allowed me to have the flexibility within my schedule to raise a family and do what I love which is to help people."

Chantel Stevens, Personal Trainer
Manhattan and New Jersey

"I have worked as a mobile trainer for 5 years. I wish I started as a mobile trainer because I spent 6 years prior to working for gyms earning $20 a session when I now earn $65.00 and am paid what I am worth."

Amanda Humphries
San Diego, California

"I started my mobile training business in 2001 and I have received great rewards. My client retention rate is much higher then the average fitness profession because I travel to them and there is no longer that excuse factor involved of they cant make it in time etc. Becoming a mobile fitness trainer has increase my income drastically.

Kent McCurdy
Denver Colorado

"When I got involved in mobile fitness training I was a bit skeptical because I was concerned I would spend all day traveling and less time actually training. After I applied my business plan I was able to isolate a specific area of town and it takes me 10 minutes of travel time at most. I also like it because it gives me that 10 minutes between clients to recharge and make phone calls if necessary."

Lisa Conz

Western Mass

Preface

This is the third book in "The Success Express" series. These books have been written specifically to educate and help guide the fitness professional who desires to be an independent business owner through the mine field of pioneering and then sustaining a company.

The first book, *"Launching Your Very Own Fitness Company"* assists in setting up the business infrastructure necessary to grow the enterprise, minimize liability, handle taxation and other business-specific issues. Having accomplished that first and critical step, its now necessary to start earning some money! Book two *"90 Days to a FULL Client Base"* is a comprehensive plan for acquiring clients and attaining financial viability.

With the two foundational issues of the first two books taken care of, this (and subsequent) books in the series present specific plans for launching and growing divisions or profit centers that will exist within the organization.

"The Fitness Entrepreneur" will provide education and a specific business plan for launching a successful mobile fitness business. That is, providing fitness services on an "I come to you" model. This business model has many advantages and should be considered by anyone desiring to become an independent business owner in the fitness industry, but especially those looking to get into business with limited financial resources. A key advantage of the mobile services company is its relatively low overhead/start-up costs and equally low operating expenses.

Also provided in this book are numerous examples of business and marketing plans. These practical, hands-on pages will prove invaluable for those who want to not only read but actually get started making this enterprise a reality. Forms providing complete structure are available in the appendix. Just copy and fill-in the requested data to get started developing business.

Contents

Chapter Four

Chapter One

Mobile Fitness Training

A Definition

Before tackling any topic it's important to first define exactly what's being discussed. For the purposes of this book, "mobile fitness training" simply means training clients in a location that does not require payment of rent or a high overhead. This can be done in several ways. It can be working with clients in the privacy of their home, in their office or residence gym (the latter meaning a common-use gym facility, as opposed to inside their personal dwelling), even in a local park. If there is no rent or fees to be paid, then that's a location that qualifies. Where ever the location — the crux of the business model is, "I come to you".

Does no rent or major investments mean more profits?

In most cases, yes! The information provided in this book will enable just about anyone to get a mobile fitness business off the ground and running with a very small initial investment amount. As a mobile fitness business owner it's possible to run the business out of your home, public-use land and/or facilities and a multitude of other easily accessed sites. As you'll discover in the pages of this book, mobile fitness training is not only a lot of fun, it's a great way to stir one's creative juices as a fitness professional and is one of the best ways to generate substantial income as mobile services do not require a major investment to get launched and have very limited overhead. A much larger percentage of the sum billed the client stays in the trainer's pocket—and that's nothing but a good thing.

Pros and cons of mobile fitness training

First let's make a very important concept perfectly clear; a personal trainer who has a personal client base is not a business owner. This is a solo fitness trainer. Personal trainer Susie may have 10 in-home clients and a small boot camp she runs in Balboa Park two mornings a week, but that does not instantly make her a business owner. She will have some basic business functions which need to be properly run in order for the client base to stick around but she is not running a business, she's just working with clients. She graduates to business owner when she begins to bring aboard independent contractors or employees, begins to market the company rather than just her name and what she has to offer, and she branches out to offer multiple services and/or products.

As with any business, it's critical to weigh the pros and cons of becoming a mobile fitness trainer or opening up a mobile business, before actually doing it. Table 1.1 is a non-comprehensive list constructed by our staff of trainers at Achieve Fitness USA of some pros and cons they have encountered. The Achieve Fitness USA staff has over 300 years of experience collectively in the mobile training arena and have seen scores of trend changes, faced various economic realities and generally have a superior understanding of what it takes to survive in the mobile fitness training business.

Table 1.1

Pros	Cons
Self Determination You are the boss. There's no clock to punch and no one making you show up at work each day.	**Self Determination** You are the boss. There's no clock to punch and no one making you show up at work each day. (more on this apparent dichotomy later)
Higher Earnings There's no gym or facility taking a percentage of the cut, profit margin per session is much higher.	**Life's On the Road** You don't have the convenience of being at one location. No set location to market, to have signs for, etc.
Client Retention Mobile trainers tend to retain clients an average of 4 years longer than those in traditional gyms. Because you go to the client, it's easier for them to keep you.	**Finding Clients** Though finding clients is not particularly difficult (read "90-Days to a FULL Client Base), clients aren't a captive audience like in a traditional gym.
Set Your Own Hours Not a morning person? Ok. Don't want to work on Sundays so you can spend time with family? Ok. You call those shots.	**Often Work With Limited Equipment** Some clients might have little or no fitness equipment. In these cases you're limited to what fits into your car.
Travel Time Unlike working in a gym, in-home training provides (down) time in between clients. This time can be put to productive uses	**Travel Time** Since you travel to the client, there is down time, aka: unpaid time, every day. Though the drive time is not billable, the gas still costs money.
Fewer Cancellations In-home trainers do get fewer cancellations and no-shows. One reason for this is elimination of the "caught in traffic" excuse.	**Higher Vehicle Expenses** Assuming you're driving, being mobile places more wear and tear on a car. Fueling and regular maintenance, like oil changes, occur with greater frequency.

There are some important statistics to know and to understand as you consider venturing into the mobile personal training industry. No one should embark upon this endeavor without the realization that this is going to take grit, determination and hard work. But for those smart few who decide to venture out into these waters, the rewards can be quite fulfilling. From our own experiences and industry sources:

- 82% of clients trained in-home stay with the trainer longer than 2 years. In contrast about 8% of clients who train with a trainer in a gym stay with that trainer for longer than 1 year. Percentages are far better for training clients in- home.

- In-home personal trainers receive 37% more referrals than health club trainers.

- In interviews, in-home personal trainers consistently report they are much happier with their careers than in-gym trainers.

- According to National Trainers, on average mobile trainers retire 42% sooner than traditional employee and/or subcontracted personal trainers.

Speaking in general terms, the fitness field is a phenomenal place to carve out a living. And all indications are that things will only get better. According to IDEA Health & Fitness the personal training industry grew 21% from 1996 - 2000 and continues to grow (not so coincidentally) with the United States obesity rate which has increased every year for the past ten years!

Referencing "Fastest Growing Occupations Requiring Post-Secondary Training", "Fitness Trainer" is #3 and expecting 44% growth by the year 2012!

And, "Occupations with the Largest Employment Requiring Post-Secondary Education", "Fitness Trainer" is #10 in the category "Fastest Growing Occupations ".

So there's little doubt that the fitness industry is a hot place to be. The questions are, "Is it for you?" and if so, what form of occupation do you really want? Proving mobile fitness services is but one niche to dwell in, and it's a good one. But understand that nothing is all roses. Study Table 1.1 and determine for yourself if the pros out weigh the cons for your own situation. For the authors they certainly have. We left the heath club scene, have never looked back and don't regret the decision for a moment.

Before getting started

First off, honestly answer this question, "Why do I want to be a mobile fitness trainer?" It's a question that's both simple and complex at the same time. Go through the pros and cons (Table 1.1) and answer this question. Should you determined this occupation and lifestyle is for you fill out the form below and spend some time with it. Table 1.2 contains an abbreviated set of questions that a prudent person should ask him or herself prior to starting a mobile fitness business. The answers provided are just samples, designed to stimulate your thought processes. Create a blank version of this table and fill it in with your own responses. Over the years we've discovered that self analysis of this sort is a very useful investment of time.

Table 1.2 - Why do I want to become a mobile trainer?

Reason I want to be a mobile fitness trainer	What if anything is in my way of doing this?	How can I overcome the obstacles in my way?
Pride of ownership	My other job	I will deduct hours at other job as I increase hours here.
Opportunity to set own hours	My wife is not supportive	I will discuss with her how this is my dream and gain her support
Be able to manage other trainers	Time	I have 2 children, but, I will work from home so I can be around them more
I can grow the business as big as I want it to become	I need more knowledge on how to grow and manage a business	Read excellent books and educate myself on how to becoming a successful entrepreneur
Job Satisfaction	Lack of organization	I will plan each day in advance and use a *time management chart
For both physical and emotional satisfaction	I am currently over weight	I will put into practice what I have learned about conditioning the body

*A sample time management chart may be found in the appendix

Business Plan and Development

Mobile fitness services is a great business to be in. Earnings are generally higher than club-based and the pros usually out weigh the cons by a fairly wide margin. The list above is strictly meant as food for thought. Most readers will be able to go through the cons and find most not relevant to their personal situations. Next, go to page 40 for an example of two business plans and take a close look at the business plan for mobile fitness training and opening a gym or studio. Compare the investment amounts, opportunities and effort necessary to develop this business. Reviewing these business plans can open your eyes not just to the opportunity available but will also demonstrate the effort necessary in organizing what we call VGB. VGB stands for Vision, Goals and Business. In our capacities as business coaches VGB is the process we advise clients follow to get an execution plan in place which then leads to acquiring and pursuing business. There will be more on VGB later but for now take a close look at the two business plans provided, use them to make decisions concerning whether this business is right for you.

Should you reach the conclusion that a mobile fitness services business is one you want to be in, we believe you have made an excellent choice, but don't be fooled. Opening a great mobile personal training business (or department within a larger business) takes a lot of time, effort and determination. But once its functional clients stay longer, you earn considerably more money on a per session basis, and as word gets out you'll quickly realize the opportunity to turn a solo mobile training company into a complete business.

Understand that there is no substitute for effort. Opening a business is no easy task and although this is one of the most profitable opportunities in the fitness industry, it requires complete dedication. As with anything, giving 30% effort will result in 30% returns. If you haven't already, purchase and read *"90 Days to a FULL Client Base"* to learn how to develop your client base and that of other trainers you hire. Both activities are key components to growing the business. Order *"90 Days"* at www.funfitpro.com.

Leverage your mobile training business to expand
One nice thing about starting as a mobile trainer is the ability this business platform provides for expansion. If a goal is to open a fitness studio, gym or corporate fitness business — mobile services is a natural feeder into the business lines. Making the move into any of these is a somewhat natural progression. As you develop the mobile training company you are also developing important business relationships, partnerships and other contacts. Not to mention clients. Most fit pros who open a studio or gym do so with few or no clients and must build clientele from the ground up. With a successful mobile services company, you are likely to have a full list of clients in-waiting. As soon as the doors to your studio open, there are already 10, 20, maybe 50, 100 or more people ready and waiting to begin training with you (and/or your training staff) in the new facility. It's a nice side perk and even more motivation for those who have the goal of ultimately owning and running their own gym.

Great business minds understand that networking is one of the major keys to success. Relationships made while running the mobile company can and will be feeding clients into the gym for years to come. When we opened the first studio in Denver Colorado, Robert had a mobile training division in place for three years. The first day the studio opened there were clients and business partners referring new members immediately. The studio became successful because of the mobile fitness training division.

Realize that how you conduct yourself and your business today affects everything tomorrow. By effectively running a company and developing great networking relationships you can set yourself up for success in the future as expansion and growth opportunities into other markets present themselves.

Opening and running a business is not easy in any industry, but with hard work and determination, reaching financial independence is within anyone's grasp. One of the greatest feelings in the world is when you reach the point that the business can support your life and you do not need to actually be putting in working hours to earn an income. To reach this particular life goal, ownership is the only way to go. And a mobile fitness company is one of the best to own due to low barriers to entry, limited exposure and risk. The initial investment amount is nil and there is no hefty purchase or lease payments for equipment. As the proprietor, there's no reason to take on massive debt to get started.

Chapter Two

Getting Open for Business

We once worked with an accountant who gave some very interesting, very telling advice about opening and running a business. This accountant said something very profound, he said, "Treat this business just like a baby. It needs love and nurturing. Your job is to provide for and assist in the growth and development of this baby. A business needs the same care and love. And just as with a baby, there is a daily lifestyle change that must occur in order to become successful. You must truly love your business and provide it what it needs day in and day out."

As everyone knows, there will be both good days and bad. One important business goal must be not allowing bad personal days to negatively affect the business, and vice versa. This is a difficult personality trait to cultivate but as you begin to master it you'll inevitably grow business faster and be happier in your personal life as well. Always remember, the company has your traits, ethics and beliefs—but it is a separate entity must be treated like one.

Common mistakes

The statistics regarding the number of fitness professionals who go into business for themselves and fail are quite sobering. By some industry sources as many as 92% go belly up and close the doors within two years. As a business owner in the fitness industry you want to avoid becoming another in this long line of negative statistics.

Since so many try opening a fitness business and fail, it stands to reason there must be some common reasons why. Below is a list of some of the most common reasons we've seen fitness professionals lead very short careers as business owners.

- Hastily going into business
- Lack of focus
- Lack of on-the-job experience
- Inadequate research and testing
- Absence of a well thought-out business plan
- Lack of working capital
- Unprofessional decor, theme, logo, stationery, attire, packaging, ads and web site
- Untrained staff
- Poor relationships with vendors
- Unfocused (or non-existent) marketing plan
- Not using advertising media that works best for the specific business
- Skimping on insurance
- Failure to recognize potential problems before they become real ones
- Inadequate networking and business relationship building skills
- Undisciplined daily activities
- Not recognizing limitations and staying within them

On the other side of that same coin, here is a list of common reasons for success. Or, put another way, activities that will help anyone to avoid the pitfalls listed above.

- Development of an effective mailing list
- Watch for growth possibilities and plan growth direction

- Stay current by joining trade associations, subscribe to and read trade magazines
- Continue to review, develop and update the business plan
- Able to state, specifically, how you will market your service business
- Develop a detailed budget, include proposed expenses for displays, signs, advertising, promotions and web site marketing, etc.
- Maintain a file for merchandising and marketing ideas
- Take seminars and classes for both training clients and business knowledge
- Attend openings and promotions of businesses like yours.
- Develop and maintain an employee handbook
- Talk to anyone and everyone in your field
- Collect business cards
- Prepare a plan for growth
- List potential problems and possible solutions
- Become personally involved in selling your service
- Keep a journal to record business experiences

Initial investment

One of the most common questions we hear from want-to-be or soon-to-be business owners is, "What should my investment be when I first open my fitness training company?" The answer is, there is no specific answer. There are tons of variables that need to be taken into consideration and naturally, everyone's situation is a little bit unique. The initial investment could easily run into the tens of thousands of dollars just to set your self up as a corporation, develop and run print advertisements, and have everything reviewed by an attorney for legality.

If you have the financial resources available, then it's certainly easier to take some calculated risks in the arenas of marketing and advertising. Or you can take the minimal investment route and spend next to nothing on advertising but try to grow by networking and partnering. Or come down somewhere in the middle.

One of the beauties of opening a mobile training business is cost factors can be very minimal. There's no facility rent to be paid, no expensive equipment to purchase or lease, no water or electric bill, etc. If you are able to market yourself and can learn how to train clients with a minimum of equipment (training clients with very little equipment will be covered in a later section) you'll be able to start and grow the business with a minimal investment.

Pay careful attention to the business plan examples in this book and look at the sample financials for starting the fictitious business. This will give a clear picture of what it will take to open your mobile training business. Then look at the cost factors involved in opening a fictitious gym. This will allow for a comparison of each business model and provide solid information for making an educated decision.

Maximize earnings with multiple revenue streams
Opening a mobile fitness business is taking the low investment route into the fitness training industry. We generally expect new business owners in this niche to be profitable in about 90 days - assuming you're training some clients, working to hire independent contractors and employees and growing a vendor system – all of which are outlined throughout this book. Doing this provides the opportunity earn more income initially, with the goal of having a full client base then hiring trainers to work for you and duplicate your success. Initially your success is

dependent upon your ability to pick up clients. Read *"90 Days to a FULL Client Base"* to master this essential skill. Then pass the expertise on to your staff, thereby growing your company.

As a mobile training business owner there are multiple services that can and should be offered to maximize income potential. Private training, semi-private training, small-group, bootcamps, kids camps and online fitness coaching just to name a few. Having more than one source of income is critical especially in the formative months and years of your business. Having all of one's income tied to personal training services exclusively can be a deadly mistake. If, for whatever reason, several clients drop you at the same time—you're in for a lean month or months. Trainers with this kind of business typically have an income chart that resembles a rollercoaster. This month they earned $5,000, but last month $3,300, the month before that $6,500 but the one prior $1,950. However if income is being gleaned from three or four different sources, one underperforming this month can be offset by others still pulling in money.

A great business owner maximizes opportunities to earn income. Do this by offering multiple revenue streams. And remember, we're talking about a mobile fitness services company. Each of the business mentioned above can be performed in-home, outdoors or in other rent-free areas. Do this by having a great organization process which includes a quality rate card (see the example rate card in the appendix) a website, e-newsletter and marketing materials that list all available services and pricing. A good rate card should incorporate all available revenue streams. Having a professional rate card is very important, it lends an air of success and professionalism. At this point a quality website and newsletter are assumed. If you don't have one or both, it's past time to get started. Both will be essential to building your mobile fitness company. Here is a non-exhaustive list of potential revenue streams that can be incorporated into your business;

- Fitness evaluations and program design
- Hiring trainers and independent contractors to work with clients you cannot or do not choose to work with
- Women's only camps
- Injury rehabilitation programming
- Product and/or equipment sales
- Small-groups and bootcamps
- Online fitness coaching
- Life coaching
- Sports performance/enhancement training (plyometrics, etc.)
- Maternity and post natal programs
- Weight loss programs or camps

You can offer any fitness related services that do not require rent or a facility use charge. Of course some of these businesses may require a more substantial investment in equipment but at least those are one-time expenses, not like rent which recurs each and every month.

By offering all these services we have now created multiple revenue streams which means we can maximize our earning power from each client. This means a client might come aboard and do private training but decide to buy a mobile training fitness kit. I have set up the partnership (as explained in section IV) to have the fitness kits shipped from an equipment company, I charge the customer and take a $100.00 profit. This allows us to earn a free $100 by setting up relationships and not just referring clients to buy somewhere else.

Another excellent way to add revenue streams is to incorporate product and/or equipment sales, so when your mobile clients need dumbbells, resistance bands, stability balls, etc., they can purchase them directly from you rather than a fitness retail store. Or, when working with a married man or woman offer a plan where they can add the spouse for an additional $10 or $20 per session. Vitamins and other nutritional supplements offer another potential revenue stream. A smart strategy is to create a list of potential additional create income sources, place them into a chart, then develop a timeline for incorporating them into the business structure. Table 2.0 presents some possible revenue streams and ways to incorporate them.

Table 2.0

List of potential additional revenue streams	How to incorporate into the business
Partner Training	I am going to offer clients an additional person offer of $20 per session. My goal is to add 10 new clients thereby creating an additional $200 a month.
Offering mobile clients equipment	I will develop a relationship with an equipment store or manufacturer and resale equipment to clients.
Hiring independent contractors or employees	I will hire and earn $15 per each session completed by my trainers. My goal is to have 2 trainers doing 100 sessions per month earning me an additional $1500 a month.
Nutrition referral program	I will refer all my clients to Amy Westcott, certified dietician who has offered me a $75 referral fee.
Massage therapy referral program	I will refer my clients to Anna Hampton, certified massage therapist who has offered me a $50 referral fee.

When it comes to developing additional revenue streams, think out of the box. It's surprising the number of legitimate money-making ventures creative thinkers have come up with and managed to build into the fabric of their businesses. Keep it focused and keep it within fitness, but the term "fitness" encompasses a pretty broad spectrum. Go to the appendix and use the form there to begin thinking of creative ways to earn money in the business. List them even if you have no intention of pursuing the opportunity at this moment. It's important to have a list that can be re-visited from time to time.

How to determine rates

Figuring out pricing and rates can be challenging. Charge too much and the competition kills you, too little and you risk developing a "bargain-basement" reputation. It's important not to under charge for many reasons. Undercharging can easily lead to a general perception of simply being the cheap training organization on the block which in turn can lead to a perception concerning the quality you have to offer.

As in most industries, customers are aware of the fact that you generally get what you pay for. If they want to hire a trainer from organization X who has no qualifications, they can do so and pay $35 a session. They'll get a junior trainer with no certification or a "cheeseball" cert, see crummy results, risk possible injury and walk away with a bad taste in their mouth. That taste reflects not only on the specific trainer in question but on our industry in general.

Such trainers and circumstances have hurt the industry considerably and they drive down the value of what we have to offer which, in our opinion, is quite substantial.

In most cases however, it doesn't pay to be the most expensive trainer on the block either. No matter how good you are you can price yourself right out of the market. When just starting a business, this is a tough line to tow. Certainly there are trainers and training organizations that make their living by cultivating a premium image and services the top end of the market. If standard local rates are $50 per session, they charge $90 and really hammer the "you get what you pay for message" hard. But for someone just getting the doors for business open, this is a very difficult business model to make work. First of all, the raw numbers are not in your favor. That is, the number of people in the community who can afford to pay these rates is limited. And this is a business model that really relies on referrals for growth. Basically, rich clients tell other people of means about your services. Since you're just starting out, you have no rich clients (or poor ones, for that matter).

We recommend you do research. Who are your competitors? Where are your competitors? What do your competitors charge? Call every training organization in the region—mobile services and gyms alike—and get quotes. Surf their websites, subscribe to their newsletters, etc. Find out what different companies charge for services and match what you have to offer up to the region's average. Don't be the most expensive, don't be the least. Find that happy medium where, financially, clients can relate to your services and you can easily justify the costs in your consultation meetings with prospective clients. For the most part we recommend coming in closer to the higher end than the lower. This tends to earn the label of a valued personal trainer, and it's hard to lose that reputation—just as it's hard to lose the reputation of being dirt cheap. In business for the past 8 years as "The cheapest feet on the street!" Tom's Discount Shoes can't all of sudden increase all prices by 40%

and boldly proclaim, "Now your premium footwear provider". That doesn't work. The reputation for being the low-cost leader is already in place. Shedding it is nearly impossible. The same is true for your business.

Drop "FREE" from your vocabulary

One of the most valuable lessons we've ever learned, and one of the most difficult to get new trainers to accept, is refusal to use the word "free". Don't de-value your services by giving things away for "free". "Complimentary" says the same thing without de-valuing your services and what you have to offer. We term the first consultation to the customer as receiving a complimentary session.

Different regions have different rates

It's very important to study the region and become an expert on what others are charging before getting started. This allows you to determine what profitability and cost factors will look like on a per session basis. Be aware that rates can and do vary vastly within a single state, sometimes within just a few miles. We see rates for mobile training in Manhattan (New York City) as high as $150 per session and as low as $65 per session in some gyms. In Manhattan, Kansas rates tend to sit around $36 per session. Our partner in Boise, Idaho bills $35 and $55 a session. Costs of living, number and dispersion of competitors, population, local median income, status of the economy (local and national) and many other factors influence rates and all must be taken into account when determining rates. Fortunately, most of this work has already been done, you just have to invest the necessary time to find, read and learn it.

Some regions are better than others

Although your services are needed and affordable to the majority of the population, it's important to research the demographics of your area. Do this by visiting www.demographics.com or doing a simple goggle search on "demographics (name of city/cities)". Research income levels, lifestyles, white collar versus blue collar jobs base, median age, median property values, average education levels, and just about anything else you can think of. And of course, the competition. In addition to helping you understand this important information when opening your business it aids in targeting specific markets.

For instance, if you are in Aspen, Colorado and the average income is $350,000 a year you're going to adopt marketing strategies and pursue partnerships capable of helping penetrate this market. If in Palm Springs, California and targeting a region rich in retirees with an average age of 71, this will require a completely different strategy, set of partners and significantly change the type of trainer you'll be looking to hire and bring into your company. A performance or sport specific specialist is probably not the ideal individual for working with a silver population. The demographics of a region can tell you a lot about how you will operate and implement the business plan.

Bain storm and try to determine ways to increase profits without much additional investment into the business. Check the following rate card, notice how we have created opportunity to earn income and grow the business by adding revenue streams. There are dozens of ways to can increase income by adding revenue centers. Determine which ones are right for you and incorporate them in your mobile fitness training business.

Table 2.1 - Example of a Mobile Fitness Training Rate Card

Service Offered	Price	Description
Personal evaluation and exercise program development	$199	Your certified mobile fitness professional will evaluate current fitness level and design a customized exercise program to reach your desired fitness goals.
Private Training Session	$65.00	45-60 minute 1-on-1 training session in the comfort of your own home.
Semi-Private Training	$85.00	45-60 minute 2-on-1 training session. Workout with a friend or spouse and save!
Classes or group training	*Quote	We offer classes and small group training sessions at various times and locations.
Just the Girls	$169 per month	Our non-intimidating women's only fitness camp meets at 7:00am on Monday & Thursday at Walter's Park.
Boot Camp	$229 per month	Join us at Hyde Park daily for a personalized Boot Camp for all fitness levels.
Kids Fitness Zone	$167 per month	Join us at Jefferson County High School on Monday and Friday for a fun fitness camps.
Consultations		Lets get together to discuss the opportunities we have to help you reach your goals.

Table 2.2 - Products and Programs

Additional	Cost	Description
Mobile fitness exercise kit	$199.95	1 fitness ball, 5 resistance bands (various resistance), 1 Bosu ball, 1 balance board
Exercise Journal	$19.95	1 personal 24-week exercise journal to record diet/calories and exercise progress
Quick-Start Program*	$249.95	1 personal evaluation, program design + 2 sessions to get you started
Results Program*	$995.95	1 personal evaluation, 1 exercise journal, 1 Results Program binder + 15 private sessions
Email accountability program	$25.00 per month	Complete easy-to-understand forms and email workout logs in. We analyze your logs daily with support only a click away.
Nutrition Counseling		Schedule an appointment with our nutrition specialists.

*These programs could require a mileage or destination charge.

*Prices are subject to change

Income expectation plan

As mentioned earlier, one reason a mobile fitness business can be successful quickly is the lack of operating overhead. The business can become profitable almost immediately in many cases. Because there is very little overhead it's possible to be profitable almost immediately.

While its true that profitability can and often does come more quickly, this is not necessarily the case in all situations and we certainly don't want to be mistaken for saying that this business is "easy". Launching a mobile fitness services company takes incredible effort, support, drive and determination.

Chart 2.0 is an "expectations chart". It's a sheet we have developed for mobile trainers who enter our local business structure. This is kind of an expectation sheet for the trainer so he or she visualize goals and has an accountability system in place. It's aggressive but not unrealistic. We highly suggest constructing something similar for yourself and for anyone you bring into the organization to work with you. Remember, vision, goals, business. Each is an important component and none will happen without some system of accountability. As the business owner you set goals and provide the tools that allow your trainers to attain them.

Expectation Chart

Chart 3.0

Service	3 months	6 months	1 year
Mobile Training	15-20 sessions per week	25 or more sessions per week	30 or more sessions per week
Boot camp	Start 1 camp with at least 5 participants	Grow camp to 10, or, start at least 1 more camp of 5	Have at least 2 camps of 10
Semi-private sessions	2 semi-private sessions per week	3 semi-private sessions per week	5 or more semi-private sessions per week
Classes	Instruct 1 class per month	Instruct 2 classes per month	Instruct 1 class per week

Evaluations	Perform an average of 4 evaluations per month	Perform an average of 8 evaluations per month	Perform an average of 12 evaluations per month
Other			
Other			
Other			
Other			
Other			

Charts like this one serve three important purposes.

- Accountability - it gives the business owner and the trainer (both of whom are the same person at first) a quantifiable measuring stick for daily activities.

- Expectations – there are no questions. Charts like this spell out in writing what is expected.

- Goals – this chart allows clear goal setting which in turn allows for a system of rewards for goals being met.

When the time comes, insert this chart or one similar to it into your business plan.

Proper business set up

Having determined that a mobile fitness training business is right for you and having made the decision to get started, there are some critical ground-laying steps that must be taken before actually going out and landing the first client.

What follows below is a brief re-creation of information covered extensively in *"Launching Your Very Own Fitness Company"*. For much more detail and specifics, we highly recommend reading it. We are not qualified to provide information on your particular state's taxation issues and codes but we can provide you with the basics on how to get started. In now way should this information replace the information that will be provided by state agencies a competent tax accountant and/or lawyer.

The first thing to do is become a legal and recognized business entity. Do that by:

- Applying for a business license. A license in most states runs between $25 and $50. Register your business as either a sole proprietorship, S-Corporation (S-Corp) or Limited Liability Company (LLC). Contact the Secretary of State's office and/or Department of Revenue as they can provide small businesses with tons of useful information.

- Register the company name as a trade name, if necessary.

- Open a business banking account in the company name. In order to properly run the business it needs to be separate from your personal income. Opening a company checking account allows tracking and various other separations of activities. (note: You can not open up a business account with a bank until you have applied for and received a business license.).

Initial investment

Once the business checking account has been opened, put in whatever dollar amount is necessary to get the business up and running. This can be as little as $5 and largely depends upon the necessary initial investment in equipment. If you have little or no equipment a few hundred dollars should be more than adequate to cover the basics — quality duffel bag, 55cm stability ball, a range of resistance bands and a few other staples of the mobile trainer.

After the business account is open, run all business funding activity through the company. Both credits/deposits and debits/expenditures. All checks from customers should be made out to the business name and not your personal name. Take care to keep everything separate and distinct.

If you plan to sell product, go to the state and apply for a resale license. In most cases this will necessitate paying quarterly sales tax or sales tax estimates. Collect sales tax directly from customers pay the state taxing authority the appropriate percentage each quarter.

Contact your local IRS department or enlist the services of an accountant and/or review the necessary information on the state website. Begin paying taxes quarterly or use a payroll service for handling employees.

Although it's self-serving, we can't recommend reading *"Launching Your Very Own Fitness Business"* highly enough. The information mentioned above is cursory at best. The second book the *"The Success Express"* series goes into great depth and detail on each of these topics and each is complex in its own right.

Listed below are several key websites to visit and surf for vital information as well.

www.irs.org
www.achievefitcoaches.com
www.businessknowhow.com
www.businessnation.com
www.businesslicenses.com
www.legalzoom.com
www.startupnation.com
www.myownbusiness.org
www.mindyourownbiz.org
www.powerhomebiz.com
www.smallbusinessstrartup.biz
www.achievefitnessusa.com
www.funfitpro.com

Chapter Three

Development of the VGB
(Vision, Goals and Business) Plan

Learning how to develop the VGB

Developing your business vision leads into development of business goals both of which then get implemented into the business plan.

- Develop business vision
- Take the vision and turn it into business goals
- Take the goals and the vision and turn them into a structured business plan

The VGB is not the only thing necessary get the business open and equipped for success, but it's one of the most important. Neglecting thorough completion of this section is a major mistake. Over the years we have seen many fitness professionals start a business and neglect this process. Sadly enough, nearly all fail. Development of a business plan is one of the most important things you can do as it not only provides a structured approach to the company, having a real plan also grants access to bank loans based solely upon the fact that one actually exists. Lenders want to know they are dealing with a professional, not just some wannabe who needs money to chase a pipe dream.

Can my business plan change?

Absolutely, but it's very important to document any and all changes to the plan in the plan. Adding new revenue streams or taking old unproductive ones out, changing hiring procedures, adding new programs, all of these justify a change to the business plan and should be documented. Having the flexibility to make changes as the business grows is important, but take a systematic approach to changes. As the business grows its only natural the plan grows also. One of the main goals of the initial business plan is to provide a necessary framework. This is helpful in monitoring daily activities to be certain everything is directed toward growth or other productive means. Over the years there will be many occasions when parts of the plan must change or adapt. Keep the business model current and under control, the diligence now will pay off later.

Developing vision and goals

A great way to develop your vision and goals is to start by asking critical questions. The questions presented in this chapter are made to inspire thought about the ultimate configuration of the business and lead to a more clear picture of the vision and goals. Answering the following questions will help start goals development and implementation of the goals into the business plan. Feel free to answer these questions in a general nature then come back later when you can provide better, more detailed answers. It's very important to answer all questions to the best of your ability. The vision and goals questionnaire is designed to help provide a clear picture while sculpting goals. The goals will then be implemented into the business plan later.

Vision and Goals Questionnaire

(To be completed before starting the vision,
goals and business plan sections.)

Financial questions

1. How many client sessions are necessary each month to make this venture profitable? (Obviously you must know your cost per session in order to derive this answer.)
2. What will be your total initial investment amount in this business?
3. What is the goal date for 100% recovery of the initial investment amount?
4. What is your current breakeven point? In other words, how much money do you need to generate right now to make ends meet?
5. What specifically will you have to do to get there?
6. What will your rate sheet look like? How much will you charge for various services?
7. How and when will monies be paid and what is your billing process? (Will you invoice clients monthly, by the session, etc.? A sample of an excellent billing form may be found in the appendix. Reproduce and private label it to your own business.)
8. Will you accept credit cards?
9. What steps must be pursued in order to facilitate a merchant account for credit card processing?
10. Will the business produce any immediate income?
11. Is there income from other sources? (Another part-time job, etc.)
12. If not available as cash on hand, how will you find the capital to meet initial costs?
13. What plan of action will you take if income doesn't meet your operating costs?
14. Will you have an office or other facility requiring rent?
15. If so, how much can you afford?

Marketing and advertising questions

1. What specific marketing activities can you commit to right now?
2. Do you plan on paying for advertising, if so where and how much?
3. What numbers, both in terms of people and dollars, do you anticipate the marketing and networking you commit to will generate? (If you have no clue, that's ok, just guess.)
4. What will you do if that marketing doesn't pull the numbers you expect or need? (What is the alternative plan?)
5. What obstacles do you anticipate and how will you overcome them?
6. How will people find out about your business in the next 30 days?
7. How will you brand your company name?
8. Will you do mailings? If so, to whom? What are printing and postage costs?
9. Will you invest in a logo, shirts, or uniforms? What is the associated costs?
10. What other sources of revenue (profit centers) will you have? List each and how you plan to pursue them.

If, in looking these questions over, you find yourself totally or even partially perplexed, if you're not entirely sure what justifies "marketing activities", see chapter 5 *"Develop a Marketing Vision and Message"* in *"The 90 Day Success Express"*. You will find it invaluable.

Customer service and time management questions

1. How will you motivate and retain clients?
2. What is your guarantee?

3. What specifically will clients receive for their investment in you?
4. How will you handle dissatisfied clients?
5. Who will do the bulk of the service? Is it only you, or will you be bringing in employees and/or independent contractors?
6. How will you manage employees or independent contractors? (Daily face time, weekly managers meetings, daily email check in, etc.)
7. What does your customer service plan look like? (Follow up by telephone with clients in need, mail customer satisfaction forms, online survey, etc.)
8. How will you find time to follow up on prospects who inquire about your service?
9. Do the commitments you're making here leave sufficient time for marketing?

Ok, you've completed the vision and goal development questionnaire. You've answered many important questions. As you are developing the vision and goals for your company be sure and consider how you answered each question and how those answers relate to the structure of the enterprise.

Develop the business vision

In starting a business the importance of developing a business vision cannot possibly be overstated. Think of this business venture as a journey, a road-trip of sorts. One sure way to get lost, frustrated and waste a lot of fuel is to not know where you're going. There has to be a destination or what's the point of ever leaving home?

On the other hand, let's say you've left home and are bound for my place — but you don't know where I am. So you call my cell phone and ask, "Hey, how do I get to your house?" What's the first thing I'm going to ask? "Well where are you now, fool?!" If I don't know where you currently are and, more importantly, if *you* don't know where you are, how are you ever going to find your way to me? That's the purpose of the VGB.

Now that the vision and goals questionnaire has been completed, (if you skipped this step, stop, go back and do it now) its time to begin work on developing the vision for your company. Be certain you have answered the previous questions honestly and to the best of your ability. The questions are meant to spur creative thinking, which is an important component to any business beginnings.

Next we begin work on developing the mobile training business vision. Put in its simplest possible terms, how do you view your company currently, in the near and longer term future? The next section is a workbook designed specifically to help develop your business vision. Develop the business vision *before* opening the company! Many small-business owners get side tracked and run off on tangents that ultimately result in the destruction of the business. This lack of focus is potentially deadly. Develop the vision and remain loyal to it. Generally speaking, any activities that do not lead directly to advancing the company toward the vision are time wasters. And time is simply too valuable of a commodity to waste.

If the vision changes during growth phases of the company, that's great and for the most part, to be expected. But it has to be incorporated into the vision to avoid you getting side tracked and spending precious hours on an activity or activities that ultimately are not a part of the business vision.

We've seen numerous great fitness professionals not make it as solo business owners because they have no idea how to identify and avoid this particular issue. Lots of activities that seem relevant on the surface are, in fact, non-essential time wasters. For example, a number of years ago we hired an exceptional trainer and all around great guy. He was one of the first trainers in the Denver region (which is currently our flagship market) and he quickly moved into a management position and was responsible for a significant portion of the Denver business. He was smart, very high energy and had a tremendous looking future with the organization. He rocketed to over 100 training hours a month in his first 6 months and was working with management to help hire other trainers and grow the business. He was on track for a tremendous profit-sharing plan which would've meant big money. But.

At the same time as working on growing Achieve Fitness USA, he was also working on growing a multi-level marketing company. In his spare time he was hosting meetings, attending meetings, selling shampoo, laundry soap and other items to his downline and working on recruiting and growing his downline. This isn't to say that all multi-level marketing companies are no good, that's certainly not accurate, but it was a massive time-drain and distraction from the vision of developing his training business.

Although he made our company better and more profitable it was inevitable he would not be able to handle everything he was taking on. There's just not enough hours in a week to do both and very quickly he became frustrated. He ended up in the deadly trap of being mediocre at three or four things, rather than excellent at one. One day he walked into the corporate office, dropped a letter of resignation and walked out. No one can multi-task that effectively. So he decided to abandon the vision (for his fitness company) and pursue opportunity B.

He lost focus on the vision, was side-tracked by a massive time-waster and was spreading himself too thinly. The moral of this story — don't do the same. Spreading yourself too thinly is a recipe for problems. Stay on focus, stay on point. As you grow the business and realize you cannot keep up with the daily demands, hire others, monitor them closely and learn to delegate. But don't lose track of the vision. Business vision helps organize thoughts and sharpen plans so you do not make the fundamental mistake of putting your eggs into too many baskets. It's impossible to move fast enough to keep them all properly incubated, and then you risk none of them one day hatching.

How to develop the business vision

Develop your business vision by honestly describing how you see the business when it is fully mature. Everyone who opens a business has an internal picture of what the business will look like "one day". We want to paint that picture in excruciating detail. Begin that process by completing the survey below. This survey will serve multiple purposes. It will answer and organize questions that deal specifically with the true business vision. In order to do this we must first lay out the platform for your mobile training company. This vision will stick with you for years, help organize goals and set up company structure and standards. The importance of the business vision is massive. As you progress in the VGB system you'll quickly begin to understand why.

Is developing a vision like developing goals?

No, the differences may be subtle but they're important. Developing vision is based somewhat in fantasy — in a good kind of way. This is where you see the company being one day, this is dealing with growth and eventually having a business capable of delivering you to the "promise land", what ever that means to you. Maybe its financial independence, maybe retirement by age 50, or fully funding children's education funds, or purchasing a 40-foot boat with cash. These are issues of vision. Once the vision has been clarified we then begin working on and incorporating specific goals. The goals are stepping stones along the path which ultimately ends with the fulfillment of the vision. Vision provides drive and accountability over the long-haul. Goals may change and often times do, but vision remains consistent.

What if my vision changes?

If the vision changes, and this is a possibility, then the entire business plan changes with it. The business plan is based upon vision. Goals are in place to provide accountability for you as the business owner. If what you see as the pot of gold at the end of the rainbow changes, then it stands to reason that the intermediate steps toward finding that pot will change too. This is where having a business coach with whom you work on a regular basis is a good idea. Sharpen, refocus and move forward. That's what it's all about.

Developing the business vision

Type an outline of each question below and begin a mental structure or framework of what your mobile training company is going to accomplish. Use the questionnaire previously completed to provide some of the necessary answers to the following questions:

1. Describe your vision of what your mobile training company will be like (minimum of 500 words).

2. Describe where you expect the company to be 90 days after opening.

3. Describe your vision for incorporating additional revenue streams and how you will get started adding them.
4. Describe your vision of what your mobile training company will look like after one year, three years and five years.
5. Describe your vision of yourself as a fitness professional and where you envision yourself professionally in five years.

Business goal development

While answering the next set of questions keep in mind that what you put into these answers will in large part determine what you get out of the business. The questions and answers may change over the years, but developing these visions will allow you to start developing a business plan and goals.

Now that the vision is developed and the general business picture painted, its time to implement the answers to these questions into the goal section below. The next step is to break down the vision and convert it into business goals. In turn, that allows us to develop the actual business plan. Now that the vision is known, it's time develop strategies that facilitate bringing the vision to pass. The following questions are designed to stimulate this line of thinking. As you complete this section, think of where the best places would be to look for mobile training clients.

1. Where will you get mobile training clients from? (Clients can come from equipment stores, retirement homes, radio ads, etc. Be creative.)

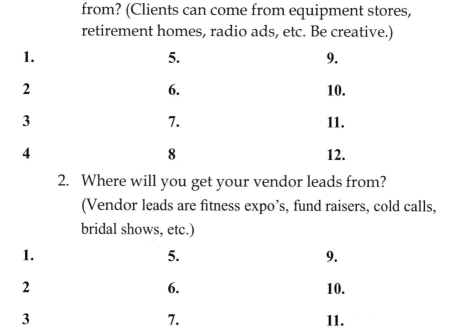

1.	5.	9.
2	6.	10.
3	7.	11.
4	8	12.

2. Where will you get your vendor leads from? (Vendor leads are fitness expo's, fund raisers, cold calls, bridal shows, etc.)

1.	5.	9.
2	6.	10.
3	7.	11.
4	8	12.

To prepare for the business plan it's necessary to turn the vision into a goal or goals. We have provided two business plan examples, one for a mobile fitness services company the other for a gym or studio. Begin by reading both and developing an understanding for how to structure your plan using these and the information gathered thus far in this book.

Take the outline in the mobile training business plan "Bodz by Julz" and use it to create your own personal business plan. The idea is to develop a complete description of the business and an organized plan for each entity within the business.

BODZ BY JULZ

Mobile Personal Training at its Best

Table of Contents

1.0 Executive Summary

Bodz by Julz will be a full-service mobile fitness company that provides a variety of catered fitness programs, specializing in personal training, nutritional counseling, personalized fitness consultations, as well as a variety of age-appropriate programs.

Bodz by Julz will be a mobile fitness training company that will start in the Denver Colorado metro area with the capabilities to expand first Denver suburbs, then south to Colorado Springs, north to Fort Collins and ultimately nation wide. This plan will be used to define the scope of services, necessary initial investment (and source), cash flow statements and other pertinent information. This plan will be used on a continual basis for evaluation of mission, goals and objectives and updated as need be.

Bodz by Julz will be a well managed, profitable enterprise that will set the standard in Denver in-home personal training. Mobile training is now the fastest growing segment of the health and fitness industry in the United States. Bodz by Julz offers a variety of programs to cater individual needs.

Mobile fitness meaning I/we will go to client sites, whether home, work or other, to provide fitness training. Health and fitness is a booming industry, producing over $11.6 billion in revenue last year and projected to continue a strong growth pattern. Mobile personal training services being just one niche in the much larger overall industry. Bodz by Julz is conservatively projecting $35,000 in profit from gross revenue of $50,000 in its first year of operation. The target is to increase both of these numbers to $55,000 and $80,000 respectively by the end of year three.

I have been a personal trainer for 15 years with a proven track record of success. My goal is to provide the community with a stable of capable, certified, knowledgeable personal trainers who provide the very best in fitness programming to clients in the comfort of their own homes. I will own, operate, hire and train the top fitness trainers, provide them with sales training, rapport development training, and be certain all trainers are properly certified and insured.

There is a great demand for mobile training. Individuals intimidated by the health club environment, who don't have time to commute to a traditional health club, or who don't want to workout alone. What ever the reasons, being mobile provides Bodz by Julz a significant competitive advantage, we remove all negativity, guide and support client's to achieving individual goals. We take the stress out of exercise and create an enjoyable venue for continuing a healthy life style.

1.1 Objectives
The principle objectives for Bodz by Julz are:
*Build personal clientele base within three months. That is, have enough personal clients to meet all of my personal (financial) obligations.
*Hire, train and have four subcontractors (trainers) also with full client bases by the end of the first year and 12 by the end of year three.
*Organize, develop and market various fitness programs (bootcamps, speed and agility camps for high school athletes, etc.) that are full to capacity.
*Sponsor and/or support at least two community events in our first year of operation.

1.2 Mission

Bodz by Julz is a professional mobile fitness training company designed to satisfy the fitness needs of individuals in the comfort of their own home. It is our mission to provide the best programs, staff, and knowledge to meet the various health and fitness needs of our clients, while generating profit for the owners. In addition to providing an excellent value to our clients, we are determined to create an unmatched workout atmosphere that will add to the enjoyment of every client and trainer of our company. Dedicated to the community, we will strive to support, sponsor and host events, whenever possible. Our hope is that through the use of our knowledge, client's enjoyment of and appreciation for health, fitness, and life will be enhanced. The company is characterized by educated, caring, knowledgeable group of service-oriented trainers.

1.3 Keys to Success

The keys to success for Bodz by Julz is our ability to effectively market, to create an unmatched reputation of success and an atmosphere where clients will be motivated and trained by qualified, certified, knowledgeable and caring trainers.

The keys to success for Bodz by Julz are:

*Successful marketing

We must make Bodz by Julz a common name in all of the areas we service by creatively marketing services to each of our target segments.

*Creating a positive atmosphere

We will enter client's homes and foster the most comfortable exercise environment possible. Our friendly, caring and knowledgeable trainers will build the rapport and relationships necessary to keep clients for years.

Providing only knowledgeable and thoroughly qualified trainers by ensuring our fitness professionals are top shelf talent who show genuine concern for the client, our clients will feel comfortable and confident in the assurance they are exercising safely and utilizing the very latest exercise science.

2.0 Company Ownership

Bodz by Julz will be incorporated. It will file under Sub-chapter S of the IRS tax code and the corporation will be privately owned. Julie Barger will own 100% of the company.

2.1 Start-up Summary

Bodz by Julz will service the entire Denver Metro area. We will advertise though Craigslist to hire personal trainers to work with clients we acquire. We will also design a web page for advertising our expertise, design and order business cards and a sign for the rear windshield of the company vehicle.

Based on the expenses outlined below, anticipated start up requirements come to approximately $900.00. Included in these costs is all development expenses, equipment, marketing/advertising, and a meager (but necessary) safety cushion. The assumptions are shown in the following table and chart.

Start-up Requirements:

Legal – $25

Filing of a DBA (Julie McGill doing business as Bodz by Julz) with the state department of revenue.

Signs - $110

Design and production of a window sign to be placed in rear windshield.

Equipment - $300

Miscellaneous items including 2 sets of yellow, green, red and blue resistance cords. 5, 8, 10, 12 and 20 pound kettlebells, balance cushion, wobble board, bodyfat calipers, tape measure, etc.

Promotional costs - $35
Design and initial order of 1,000 business cards

Safety cushion - $200
"Just in case" money I will not touch unless absolutely necessary.

Office equipment - $100
Envelopes, 2 rheems of paper, ink cartridge for printer and miscellaneous other items that will be used in the course of business.

Computer – n/a
Current computer is perfectly functional.

Cell phone - $29
Moving current 600-minute plan up to monthly unlimited minutes will cost an additional $20 per month.

Insurance - $100
Personal training liability insurance.

Personal training certification – n/a
Already have my ACE certification, those continuing education credits next year will require an investment.

CPR and first aid certification – n/a
Already have both though first aid will require re-certifying next year

Total start-up expense - $899

3.0 Services

Bodz by Julz will be an in-home personal training business that provides clients with a variety of services. A first-class fitness and lifestyle mobile training business that includes nutritional counseling, fitness consultations, beginner programs, advanced programs, maternity programs, children's programs, athletic performance improvement programs as well as programming for seniors.

Client sessions may fall into either of three categories, private (1-on-1 personal training), semi-private (2-on-1 personal training – most often a husband/wife combination), or small-group (3 or more to a session).

3.1 Equipment

All Bodz by Julz mobile trainers will be equipped with the necessary equipment for in-home training with clients who do not own home gyms. This will include, but is not limited to - jump rope, resistance bands of varying thicknesses, free weights (primarily dumbbells and/or kettlebells), 65cm stability ball, BOSU ball. Our trainers will have access to wholesale cost of any additional fitness equipment. All trainers will be fully educated on isometrics, plyometrics, a variety of resistant training programs and how this equipment is properly integrated into all such programs.

3.2 Nutrition

All trainers will be properly educated and certified on the elements of basic nutrition. This will ensure clients are receiving proper and correct education concerning health, nutrition and diet. Studies show that 70% of results are attained through proper nutrition, our trainers will be educating each and every client on the total package of health – both exercise and nutrition.

3.3 Programs

Our trainers will be completely educated on how to work with in-home clients with or with out equipment. This includes but is not limited to resistance training, isometric training, weight bearing training, plyometric training, body-weight management such as yoga and/or pilates, boot camp training and other exercise programming techniques.

4.0 Market Analysis

Because of the diversity of activities and programs available, our market segments will vary from the hardcore "work out junkies", to those just wanting a few hours a week of fun and recreation. We will hire trainers capable of working with populations from both markets and all in between.

With the number of people committing to regular exercise steadily going up, we will capitalize on both that segment of the market looking to get started as well as competitive athletes looking to improve performance.

According to statistics, revenues for the fitness industry rose from $20.7 million in 2000 to $30.6 million in 2007. This trend is projected to continue and we anticipate taking full advantage of this natural growth trend. In addition, those categorized as "frequent users" of fitness-related goods and services soared by 84% during the same period. Recent surveys cite as many as 79% of health club clients would rather train in the privacy of their own home than in fitness club. According to these industry statistics, Bodz by Julz should have a bright future.

(Reader: visit www.demographics.com and put in your local zip code(s). This website provides average incomes, average home prices and other useful demographic information.).

4.1 Market Segmentation

Clients can and will come in various shapes, sizes and ages. All clients can be placed into one of the following three categories based singularly on the frequency with which they train:

1. **Infrequent** - train once or twice times per week.
2. **Average** – train three times per week.
3. **Frequent** – train more than three times per week.

Beyond frequency, clients can generally fall into further segmentation based upon demographics and fitness goals. Examples of different client segments we will service are:

Families

These clients typically train 3 times per week. Most often this is a husband/wife duo though often there may be a child or children involved as well. A junior high or high-school aged child or children is/are the most common addition(s) to the sessions. The child or children are often times involved in scholastic athletics. These are amongst our most profitable and stable clients.

Seniors

These clients also tend to train three times per week and also are very loyal. This client segment definitely prefers one-on-one training. As health and fitness awareness increases, seniors are increasingly seeking health promoting programs and elevated levels of activity, often time at the encouragement of family and/or physicians.

Performance Improvement

Clients who are competitive athletes such as tri-athletes, marathoners and golfers occupy this segment. Or those who simply challenge themselves in the absence of others with whom they are competing (downhill and water skiers, joggers or cyclists, for instance). These athletes also represent a strong and very loyal client base.

It's important to note that a single family may well run the range of clients. For instance, mom and dad hired one of our trainers on a 20-session package as a Christmas gift for grandma who begins doing two sessions a week, (seniors, infrequent). As time went by and the relationship with grandma became strong, seeing our expertise and grandma's results, mom and dad decided it would be a good idea to hire us and begin working out themselves.

Mom and dad have a 16 year-old son who has a good shot at making the varsity football team at school next year if he really dedicates himself to working out in the off-season and puts on some speed and muscle. They hire us to design a program for the kid and work with him four days a week doing plyo and general conditioning work. (performance improvement, frequent)

Ideally we can break down 100% of our clients and place them into a category or two. Although our clientele base grows, this stays pretty consistent year-to-year. Numbers may change, but the breakdown percentage remains consistent. Knowing these numbers and managing to them is critical.

Infrequent = 20% (train about once or twice a week, often training for maintenance)

Average = 50% (train three times per week, often to lose weight and stay in shape)

Frequent = 30% (train four to five times per week and are addicted)

Families = 60% (clients find exercise important, they cherish the exercise time spent together and believe in a healthy family life style)

Seniors = 10% (clients trying to avoid the negative effects of aging process, want to maintain muscle mass and sense of balance)

Performance Improvement = 30% (train for varying reasons, but all ultimately want to become superior in their chosen endeavor)

4.2 Target Segment Strategy

We will focus our marketing strategies on those market segments that best match our offerings. Each market segment relates, in certain ways, to all the others. Our main objective with early marketing strategy will be to simply gain. Once client's experience what we have to offer and see results, they will want to participate in our programs for a life time.

Some of the ways Bodz by Julz will attract clients include:

*Promotional events at equipment stores.

*Providing (store personnel) complimentary training on new equipment.

*Hosting and/or supporting various community events that will bring clients who other wise would not come.

*Mail outs introducing our company to the community advertising complimentary nutritional counseling with training session purchased.

*Sponsorship of community runs, walks or other fitness-related events.

*Developing relationships with retailers who cater to the senior market such as hearing aid and electric wheel chair stores.

*Developing relationships with retailers who cater to the performance improvement market such as running and climbing stores.

*Offering to provide "fitness talks" to residents at local senior/ assisted living centers.

*Meeting and developing relationships with coaches and athletic directors at area high schools.

4.3 Service Business Analysis

With total reported revenue of over $10.6 billion in 2006, the sports and fitness business is a booming industry. Fitness and fitness awareness has become a part of the main stream of American thought. Although fitness clubs have been around for years, as with anything else, convenience has become a priority. As a result fitness clubs are going out of business on a daily basis. Clubs are not as convenient as a trainer to the door. This total convenience is what is driving in-home training and will propel this service aspect of the industry to record financial heights for years to come.

4.4 Competition

The competition for Bodz by Julz is slim. The only other company located in a zip code that is less than 45 minutes away from ours is "Joe Schmo Training". We believe we have found the unique marketing and growth strategy that will separate us from Joe Schmo. Joe is known for his lack of professionalism and inattention to client needs. From an examination of his website we have discovered that Joe earned his college degree less than two years ago and has been certified since last summer. He has two trainers working for him, both of whom have been certified for slightly less time than Joe has. The following table examines some key differences between Bodz by Julz and Joe Schmo.

Table 4.1

Bodz by Julz	Average Jo Shmo Trainer
Experienced trainers who provide proven results	New graduate trying to build a business
Our trainers care about clients	Only out to make a pay check
Our trainers are trained to create individual programs for all fitness levels and will research any challenge.	Most trainers create the same program for every one out of laziness and convenience.
We will be on time for each and every session	Continuously canceling or late for appointments.

We know that Joe provides services for most parts of the south metro area, mostly including Parker, Littleton, Aurora and Lone Tree Colorado. Joe charges a flat rate of $59 per in-home session and provides a 10% discount for purchases of 10-session blocks.

Because he has a calendar on his website, we also know that Joe is currently performing virtually no sessions on Tuesdays, Thursdays and Saturdays and that he currently as a once-a-week bootcamp at 10:00am on Saturdays at Gold Point County Park in Aurora.

5.0 Strategy Implementation Ideas

Bodz by Julz has a very large potential market. We will start a trend for mobile fitness training in the Denver metro area with the goal of becoming the number one mobile training services company in the home market (and eventually nation wide). This will be accomplished by actively and continuously promoting and networking as well as hosting and supporting various community events.

*Business seminars
*Body fat testing around the community, in businesses and business parks, etc.
*Equipment store seminars
*Runnin' of the Green
*Cherry Creek Sneak
*Colfax Marathon
*Bolder Boulder 10k Run
*Swim Labs Triathlon Expo
*Denver ½ Marathon
*Moonlight Classic
*Muddy Buddy
*Denver Marathon
*Harvest Moon Triathlon
*Race for the Cure
*Velo Swap
*Colorado Snow Sports Expo

5.1 Competitive Edge

The scope and variety of programs offered by Bodz by Julz are unmatched by any other mobile training company in the area. This ability to service various and diverse market segments provide an edge our current competition cannot immediately overcome. Or second competitive edge is location. Our current competition only services a relatively small segment of the Denver area — the south and southeast. By implementing an advertise and hire strategy for locating qualified trainers in all areas, we will have trainers available for every portion of Denver metro, even the more remote outlying areas.

By maintaining focus on our strategy, marketing program development and fulfillment, Bodz by Julz will be known as the only mobile fitness training firm available in a 50 to 75 mile radius. We should be aware, however, that our competitive edge may be diluted if we become complacent in our program development and implementation. It will be important for us to keep up with the current trends in both sport and fitness and seniors programming.

5.2 Sales Strategy

Sales in the sports and fitness industry are based on the services and amenities provided by the trainer. The "something for everyone" slogan fits perfectly with Bodz by Julz. All of our clients must feel like they are getting the best possible program available for their goals, budget and current fitness level.

Each potential client inquiring about training will be offered a complimentary evaluation to determine whether or not we are right for each other. During this discussion, the prospective client will be informed of all our available services and programs. Priority during this session is establishment of relationship and trust. The trainer must find compatibility with the client, if for some reason compatibility is not there, another trainer will be assigned.

In both selling our services and hiring our trainers, its passion we are hiring not just an employee. To properly promote and sell Bodz by Julz services its important to realize that to some prospects the benefits are physical, to some psychological, some are coming to us for rehabilitation and restoration of strength. What ever the case many lives are touched when a trainer is passionate about what they do. And those are the only type of trainers we will hire and the way we will effectively sell our services.

5.3 Sales Forecast

The following table and chart provides a projected sales forecast based on mid-range of prices gleaned from local competition (health club personal training rates and Joe Schmo Personal Training).

Chart 5.0

3 sessions per week	Total per week	Total per month
1 client	$180	$720
2 clients	$360	$1440
4 clients	$740	$2880
8 clients	$1480	$5920

The above figures are for personal production only. In addition to personal production we will be adding trainers and establishing a management hierarchy. In the hierarchy the manager receives $15 per session for each session his or her trainers do. Assuming a manager hires four trainers and each trainer eventually does 24 sessions per week, the following sales and income forecast can be projected for that manager:

Chart 5.1 – Manager Totals

	Sessions per week	Total per week	Total per month
Trainer 1	24	$369	$1440
Trainer 2	24	$360	$1400
Trainer 3	24	$360	$1440
Trainer 4	24	$360	$1440

In this case we can see that a manager who has successfully hired and trained four new trainers, each of whom are performing 24 sessions a week, yields an annual income for the manager of $69,120 ($1440 x 4 trainers x 12 months). This is income independent of the manager's personal production.

Once we have expanded to provide services throughout the surrounding Denver metro areas we will focus on duplicating this system in surrounding states. The company will expand and every trainer will have the opportunity to benefit from previously mentioned marketing and sales forecasting systems.

5.4 Milestone Schedule

Following is a list of important program milestones, with dates and budgets for each. The milestone schedule indicates our emphasis on planning for the future by implementation now. What the table doesn't show is the commitment behind it. Our business plan includes complete provisions for plan-vs.-actual analysis, and we will hold monthly follow up evaluations to discuss client satisfaction and new goal status.

Chart 5.2

Milestone	Start Date	Completion Date	Budget
Business plan	05/01/20xx	08/01/20xx	$0
Complete plan review	08/01/2008	09/15/20xx	$0
Financial backing presentation	10/15/20xx	01/01/20xx	$0
Company set up	09/15/20xx	11/15/20xx	$500
Logo Design	06/01/20xx	08/01/20xx	$150
Business banking account	09/15/20xx	10/01/20xx	$50
Other			$0

6.0 Management Summary

The initial management team for Bodz by Julz depends mainly on the sole owner. Julie will utilize her expertise in running the company. Her focus will first be acquiring new clients as well as new trainers working beneath her. Then helping the trainers under her build their clientele bases and teaching the trainers how to duplicate the techniques she has employed to become successful.

All of our trainers will be fully insured. There will be a contract between the trainer and client stating all clients are medically fit and waiving injury liability from us. In some case a medical clearance form, signed by a physician may be required.

Every trainer brought in will learn how to advertise and run their own business. They will also be educated on building rapport with clients, how to maintain clients and how to procure client referrals. Julie will conduct weekly training sessions with each trainer and will continue to do so until she is 100% confident the trainers will succeed.

6.1 Personnel Plan

Each trainer will be an independent sub-contractor. Their only financial obligation to Bodz by Julz will be a flat $15 fee for each session performed. The sub-contracted trainer will have the ability to determine their own pay by manipulating session rates to be congruent with the demographic and socio-economic status of the area(s) which they are servicing.

Trainers will be able to sell fitness accessories as I have developed the relationship with Fundamental Fitness Products to provide fitness equipment at or below wholesale prices. The trainer will earn 8% of the sale while Bodz by Julz earns 8%. Trainers will be able to mentor other trainers whom they in turn hire and bring in and be able to earn 3% - 5% of gross sales made by trainers they hire and mentor.

We will also advertise and conduct classes such as yoga, pilates, boot camps, sports conditioning and kids fitness classes. Bodz by Julz will have studios or other facilities set up for trainers to instruct indoor classes (and normally outdoor classes in the event of inclimate weather). The studio facilities will receive 40% and the trainer will receive 60% of gross client billings. Along with training, we will have other in-home and in-studio services available such as nutritional counseling. These services will be an added charge to the client and an up sell for the training staff.

Lastly we will have an added benefit for the trainers and an additional revenue stream they may participate in. Bodz by Julz has developed a relationship with EquipYourGym. com, an online new and pre-owned fitness equipment seller. If trainers have in-home clients who would like to acquire, add onto or upgrade equipment, our trainers may locate and procure any type of fitness equipment—from treadmills to complete gyms—and earn a commission of 10% per item sold.

7.0 Financial Plan

We are assuming start-up capital of $899 through a personal bank account. I already have a certification which is necessary not only for knowledge of proper exercise science but is also necessary for insurance purposes. (Insurance is a must.) The plan also includes expenses for basic equipment, business cards, and other necessary tools for properly working with clients and running a company. Advertising is optional but recommended to establish the company name.

7.1 Important Assumptions

The financial plan depends on certain assumptions most of which are out of our control but need inclusion never the less. Monthly assumptions are included in the appendices. From the beginning recognize that collection days are critical, but not a factor we can influence easily. At least we are planning on the problem and dealing with it. Tax rates are based on conservative assumptions.

Some of the more important underlying assumptions are; a strong economy without major recession; the rate of growth for the fitness industry will continue; no major illness, injury or other catastrophe with the potential to curb our ability to function at 100% capacity.

7.2 Break-even analysis

This analysis is base solely on client sales and immediate out-of-pocket expenses. With a start-up investment of $899 and assuming an average per-session rate of $50, we will need to sell 18 to break even (against the initial start-up investment). Considering on-going expenses such as fuel, insurance, marketing and promotional activities, etc., we need to continue selling at least sessions 26 sessions per week in order to break even on a per-month basis.

7.3 Projected cash flow Profit and Loss

A sample projected profit and loss format is depicted in Table 7.0. As a business owner your responsibility will be to plug accurate numbers into the projected P&L statement.

Table 7.0

Pro Forma Profit and Loss

Sales

Direct cost of sales

Equipment

Total cost of males

Gross margin

Gross margin %

Marketing

Telephone

Insurance

Profit

Taxes incurred

Travel expense

7.4 Projected Cash Flow

The following cash flow projections show annual amounts only. Cash flow projections are critical to our success. As a business owner, your job will be to provide accurate numbers for each of these accounting aspects. Note the differences between credit and debit items. In other words, you would add items like "Cash from Operations", however you would subtract "Other Liabilities" from the running total.

Pro Forma Cash Flow

Cash received

Cash from operations

Cash sales

Cash from receivables

Subtotal cash from operations

Additional cash received

Other liabilities (interest free)

Long term liabilities

Subtotal cash received

Cash spending

Payment of account payables

Subtotal cash spent

Net cash flow

Cash balance

7.5 Projected Balance Sheet

The balance sheet in the following table shows managed but sufficient growth of net worth, and a sufficiently healthy financial position.

Assets (right side of balance sheet)

Cash

Account receivables

Inventory

Other current assets

Long term assets

Accumulated depreciation

Total long term assets

Total assets

Liabilities (left side of balance sheet)

Notes payable

Accounts payable

Current borrowing

Other current liabilities

Total liabilities

Net Worth/Debt

(difference between assets and liabilities)

Having worked our way through an example business plan for a mobile fitness business, let's now compare the mobile fitness business plan to one for opening a gym or studio. We find it very important to give such comparisons. This provides a better overall picture. We strongly believe and as business owners ourselves, have proven, that more profit can be realized in mobile fitness training with substantially less risk than opening a gym, but seeing both sides of this coin is important.

In reviewing the next business plan be sure to notice the investment requirements and risk involved. As a business owner lowering risk should be a constant effort. And whatever risks are assumed they should be carefully pre-meditated, calculated and always come with an exit plan.

The following is a business plan for Lady USA a lady's fitness center very typical of many than can be found in cities across the country.

Lady USA
Women's Spa and Fitness

Table of Contents

1.0 Executive Summary

Lady USA will be an all-women's full service fitness center and salon located in Castle Rock, Colorado. There are currently no other facilities like this one in Castle Rock. This plan will be used to define the scope of our services, as well as the means of gaining necessary funding to open the facility. It will also be used on a continual basis to reevaluate mission, goals and objectives.

All-women's health clubs are in great demand. Many women desire to exercise in a health club environment however feel intimidated or uncomfortable by the presence of men. All-female health clubs have been in business for years with a proven track record of success. I have managed all-women's health clubs for fifteen years and find this concept to be in great demand in areas all around the expanding south-Denver metro area. With many fast growing south suburban communities such as Castle Rock, Colorado, the number of women to have health clubs such as Lady USA is steadily increasing.

My goal is to provide a comfortable atmosphere, experienced personal training and group exercise classes. Daycare will also be an asset as will being pampered with steam room , sauna, massage therapy, tanning, hair, nails and cosmetic procedures. These side amenities will be base on booth rentals payable to Lady USA by independent contractors. Both tanning and daycare will be an ad-on membership through Lady USA.

I will operate the club. I will be in the facility until it has met my standards. I will provide my staff with sales training, personal fitness training and group exercise class supervision. Members will have opportunities to participate in a variety of leisure programs and activities. The company will set the standard in the Denver metro area for women-only fitness facilities.

Women-only facilities are the fastest growing segment of the $11.6 billion health and fitness industry in the United States, growing at over twice the rate of growth for the industry in general.

In the company's mission is to offer a superior quality services it will be characterized by meticulously maintained state-of-the-art equipment and a knowledgeable, service-oriented staff. Lady USA offers weight resistance equipment, personal training, personalized fitness consultations, as well as a variety of fitness and age appropriate aerobic classes designed specifically with women in mind.

I bring many skills to the business. I have managed three health clubs for 15 years. I have been the top sales and train-the-trainer manager throughout my career, while providing an enjoyable, money-making career for each on of my staff members.

I have taught various classes, weight training programs, managed payroll, implemented many great marketing strategies that enticed women to come in. I am excellent at building a great rapport with members and will cater to those women who love great rapport and relationship with staff rather than entering the club and feeling isolated.

I believe in teamwork and will create a teamwork atmosphere to provide satisfaction to the staff as well as members. I have not only mastered inside club sales, I have also found success in corporate and outside sales and can train a small sales staff very quickly.

Lady USA specializes in training and highly personal services. This is where the rapport begins. If the members are satisfied and pampered, they refer friends. Women talk. Satisfied members are our best advertisement. The only other club in the south metro area is 24 Hour Fitness. This however is not competition. They are the fastest growing chain of fitness centers but are co-ed only. Lady of America is also present in the area. I do not see them as true competition either. While they are female exclusive, they have just one location which employs just one personal trainer. Thus they are very limited in their classes an personal training services, which does not maintain members interest. Lady of America does not provide a full service salon either.

At Lady USA members can come in and—while we care for their children—get a great workout, enjoy a relaxing steam, get a massage, then tan and relax with a facial or new hairstyle.

Marketing will be done through good demographic analysis of our surrounding communities, highly visible signage on the building, mail out coupons, radio and some television spots as well. Once the club is established, Lady USA will have an added marketing tool—word of mouth.

1.1 Objectives

The initial (financial) objectives for Lady USA are:

   * Sell 600 memberships in year one, 900 by the end of year two an 1,200 by the end of year three.
   * Organize and develop various fitness programs, such as kick-boxing classes and fat-burn bootcamps, and market them effectively so that they are filled to capacity by the end of our second complete quarter of operation.
   * Sponsor and/or support at least two community events in our first year of operation, preferably events that are especially of concern to women, like the annual breast cancer awareness walk.

Lady USA will be a success. I have a proven track record and a proven success record and our early objectives are very attainable. I feel very confident with all there is to know in opening my own all-women's health club. My goal is to provide a unique club and atmosphere to women in a fast-growing community. My full service salon, a one-stop-shop for fitness and cosmetic services, will accommodate all of their needs. The location I have chosen is ideal. It is on and directly visible from highway 84 and has at least 155,000 people passing my location every day.

1.2 Mission

Lady USA is an all-woman's, full service salon, health and fitness club designed to service the residents of Castle Rock and surrounding areas. It is our mission to provide the best programs, staff an equipment to fully meet the health and fitness needs of our members while generating a profit for the owners. In addition to providing an excellent value to our members Lady USA is determined to create an unmatched atmosphere that will add to the enjoyment of every member an employee of the facility. Lady USA strives to support, sponsor and host community events, when ever possible. Our hope is that through the use of our facility, members' enjoyment and appreciation for healthy lifestyle will be enhanced.

1.3 Keys to Success

The keys to success for Lady USA lie in our ability to effectively market the club, its programs and available amenities. We will hire qualified, certified, knowledgeable and caring trainers to work with members, run classes and coordinate programs. The specific keys to success we must manage to are:

*Marketing

We must make Lady USA a common name in Castle Rock and creatively market our services to each of our market segments.

*Atmosphere

Creating an unmatched atmosphere in Lady USA through the use and placement of first class equipment, careful selection of flooring, lighting, warm colors and textures and quality furniture in non-workout areas. Lady USA will be exceptionally well kept from a sanitation point of view and keep hours necessary to accommodate the working professionals as well as the stay-at-home mothers.

  * Knowledgeable/qualified staff

By providing members with knowledgeable and qualified staff who show genuine concern for the patrons, women will feel comfortable and confident that Lady USA will meet their fitness and beauty needs safely and professionally.

2.0 Company Ownership

In order to maximize legitimate tax deductions and to mitigate personal liability, Lady USA will be incorporated under sub-section S of the IRS tax code (S-corp). Per tax law, an S-corp must have stock ownership and a board of directors. The initial common stock distribution will be of 100 shares with 51 shares belonging to Julie and 49 to her husband, Alan. Julie will be named President of the corporation and occupy one seat on its board, Alan will be Secretary/Treasurer and occupy another.

We are going to incorporate the services of Gregory Accounting of Castle Rock to formulate and file our articles of incorporation and then will adhere to IRS standards for governance of corporations including such issues as earnings reporting, annual board meetings, etc.

2.2 Start-up Summary

Total start-up funding requirements come to $132,500. Included in these costs is facility lease, interior build out, equipment procurement, safety cushion and others. Start up cost assumptions are shown in table 2.0.

Lady USA will carry workman's compensation and liability insurance in line with industry standards for a gym and corporation of our size. Standard contracts will contain a release of liability statement that will be prepared by the law offices of Morris, Wilson and McCurdy. Members will be required to read and sign a separate waiver of liability before using tanning, daycare and spa facilities. In some cases a health history form and a medical clearance form that has been signed by their primary care physician may be required to submit (samples of both these forms can be found in the appendix of this book). Property insurance is the responsibility of the building management company, Garrett Property Management.

Table 2.0 Start-up Requirements

Legal fees - $2,500

Facility lease - $18,000 (4 months)

Signage - 1,500

Interior remodeling - $45,000

Design fees, flooring (carpet, hardwood, tile), bathrooms, walls, artwork, paint, sauna and steam room installation, front desk and offices, light fixtures, architech and builders fees, flat panel televisions, sound system, etc.

Equipment lease - $6,000 down payment

Tanning bed lease - $1,500

Office equipment - $3,000

Computers, membership tracking software, facsimile machine, etc.

Marketing/promotion expenses - $5,000

Safety cushion fund - $30,000

Two months' payroll - $20,000

Total start-up expense... $132,500

3.0 Services

In addition to being a health and fitness club, Lady USA will be a full service salon. A first class fitness and lifestyle center that accommodates massage therapy, hair and nail salon and a full compliment of walk-in/walk-out cosmetic procedures. Other amenities include a child care center, tanning, nutrition seminars, dry sauna, steam room and an attractive locker room with private showers and changing areas.

Lady USA will provide its members with qualified and knowledgeable consultants for all amenities and fully certified fully insured personal trainers and group exercise instructors.

3.1 Equipment

We will be responsible for equipment purchase and lease. All leased equipment will be procured on a lease-to-own program with a back-end dollar buy out option. Equipment is being single-sourced from EquipYourGym of Fort Worth, Texas. Initial cardio equipment will consist of five treadmills, three stair masters, ten elliptical trainers, twelve spinning bicycles and five recumbent bikes. Strength equipment will consist of two machines per muscle group (back, biceps, chest, triceps, hamstrings, quadriceps, shoulders, glutes and calves). This is 22 pieces of equipment plus benches, abdominal machines, free weights consisting of three sets of dumbbells (2lb., 5lb., 8lb., 10lb., 12lb., 15lb., and 20lb.) and weight "trees" for storage and four benches capable of both inclining and declining. In addition we will offer the following classes no less than twice per week – step aerobics, spinning, yoga, Pilates and kick boxing.

Lady USA's gym will match or exceed any other in the city. When a new member signs up she will be given a thorough tour of the facility and a complimentary training and orientation session with one of our personal trainers. Following this introductory session the member will have the option of continuing personal training sessions for the club rate of $60 per hour or $35 per half hour. The club will retain 60% of revenues generated from personal training with the remaining 40% going to personal trainer.

The fitness facility will be run by a certified strength and conditioning specialist (CSCS) who in turn be responsible for hiring and training a staff of trainers and group-x instructors. This person will report to and work directly me, the president of the corporation and general manager of the facility. Duties will include, but will not be limited to, general supervision, personalized training for members, program development and clinics, as well as aiding in marketing and promoting training services.

3.2 Tanning

Initially we will install three horizontal tanning beds which members may reserve 10, 20 or 30 minute blocks of time up to one week in advance. Tanning will be available to both the general public via tanning-only memberships as well as to full members. Tanning-only memberships will be developed, marketed and sold at a pre-determined price sometime in our second quarter of operation, however that price is yet to be determined. Tanning-only membership prices will be in a competitive range with our principle competitors in the market, Executive Tan and Sunspring Tanning. It is hoped that tanning memberships will ultimately become a feeder mechanism for selling full memberships.

Full members may use tanning beds at a cost reflective of the industry standard. Lady USA will charge full members $19.95 per month for tanning.

3.3 Cosmetic Services (hair and nails)

This service offering will be crucial in providing the desired atmosphere Lady USA intends to create. An area for hair and nails will be located in the atrium of the facility and these services will be available to both the general public and members of Lady USA on an appointment or walk-in basis, at the discretion of the service provider.

Lady USA corporation will receive a flat rate booth rental of $500 per month per unit. Julie will interview applicants and will oversee operations to ensure service quality is meeting standards, however with the exception of dictating hours of operation, these service providers will be truly independent. The presence of these amenities helps establish Lady USA as a true "one-stop-shop" for health, fitness and beauty needs, a fact that will be prevalent in all marketing materials.

3.4 Massage Therapy

Our massage therapy clinic will be located adjacent to the locker room facility so members will have a degree of privacy and easy access to their clothing. This service will also be available to both the general public and Lady USA members, with the latter receiving a 15% discount for services provided. A cost reflective of current local and industry standard will be applied. At this point competitive pricing is approximately $.90 per minute.

Massage therapy will also be a sourced to an independent contractor via monthly rental of $500 per month.

3.5 Childcare

Our daycare facility will be up to all state and local code requirements including maintaining the necessary staff-to-children ratios. We will provide services for children in between the ages of 6 months to 12 years. The daycare facility will be equipped with games, puzzles infant swings and walkers, books, coloring books and crayons, two tables and eight chairs (in appropriate children's sizes), miscellaneous toys a 27-inch television with educational and rated-G DVD's only.

Daycare will be available to members as an add-on to memberships for $19.95 per month for a maximum of five daycare hours per week or members may prepay $179 for a full year (also limited to five hours per week). Daycare may be purchased by non-members on an a-la-carte basis (those coming to the facility for tanning, hair or other services).

All daycare employees must undergo a criminal background check and a thorough reference check. Daycare hours will be 6:00am – 9:00pm Monday through Thursday and 8:00am – 6:00pm Friday through Sunday.

3.6 Proshop

A pro shop will be strategically placed near the entrance to Lady UA in order to attract impulsive buyers. Users will pass through the pro shop upon entering an exiting the facility. The pro shop will sell sports shoes, apparel, supplements and fitness accessory items such as resistance cords and pilates balls. Product for the proshop will be procured through our relationship with Fundamental Fitness Products of Denver, from whom we may purchase product en bulk at wholesale pricing. Julie will maintain inventory records for the pro shop and front desk staff will be responsible for daily sales, cleaning and necessary service.

4.0 Market Analysis

Though Lady USA will be the only female-only, full service gym salon and spa Castle Rock, the facility will cater both to Castle Rock residents and residents in surrounding communities in an approximate 20 minute radius. (Beyond that radius other south-Denver all-female facilities are available.)

From 1997 – 2007 gross revenues in the fitness industry rose from by approximately $10 billion, with a large portion of that increase being accounted for by middle-aged women. This trend is projected to continue. Frequent users of the fitness industry (those utilizing an exercise facility at least twice per week) soared by 84% during the same period. Recent surveys of over 360 fitness clubs identified the eight most profitable programs: classes, tanning, cosmetics, massage, daycare, pro shop, hot yoga, juice bar. Lady USA will offer six of these eight, including the top three.

Because of the diversity of activities and programs available, our market segments vary from exercise to those who just want a few hours of fun and recreation to those looking for someplace close to home for a weekly nail appointment. Castle Rock is predominantly a commuter center, populated by professionals who work in the greater Denver urban area. At $68,112 the mean household income is nearly $20,000 greater than the national average. We also exceed national averages for education level. Working professional women and stay-at-home wives of working professional (white collar) men make up the build of our target segment. They are educated, typically between 31 – 55 years of age, have more than one but fewer than five children and have enough discretionary income to afford membership at Lady USA.

4.1 Market Segmentation

Considering the demographic makeup of our target market, these individuals can further be sub-divided into five categories and each of those categories analyzed for likely growth over the next three years. This breakdown appears in Table 4.0:

Table 4.0

Group	Year		
	20xx	20xy	20xz
20% Competitive athlete	120	200	240
25% Recreational athlete	180	300	360
30% Health/Fitness maintenance	150	250	300
15% Group-X junkie	90	150	180
10% Silver citizens	60	100	120
Total	600	1000	1200

Competitive athlete

An important market segment for Lay USA, these women compete in tennis tournaments, 10k runs, triathlons, etc. They don't like to be locked up into long-term commitments as they want to begin and terminate their training regimens to suit the competition schedule. They like the freedom to come and go when necessary. These women are frequently quite particular about the type of workout equipment they use and follow a very regimented workout plan. For this reason they are not the best candidates for personal training as they view their requirements as being above the "general conditioning" a trainer provides. These people will be a target market for special promotions, periodic activities and a-la-carte memberships.

Recreational athlete

These athletes are dedicated to fitness programs so they can perform at their best in their chosen endeavors such as hiking, climbing, running or golf. However these activities are not competitions which require an entrance fee and typically months of physical preparation. These ladies simply like to go out and play a round of golf on Saturday afternoons and want to be in shape so their game doesn't suffer. As long as the right equipment and classes are available, these women are willing to lock into long-term commitments with a facility and are excellent prospects for personal training services.

Health/Fitness maintenance

These women enjoy being in the gym for both physical and social reasons. They are not seeking to participate in any sort of athletic competition but rather are simply aware of the many benefits of regular exercise and just want to take care of themselves. They would rather be in a gym than exercising at home alone and will do so provided the facility is well appointed, clean, not overly crowded and can be joined for a reasonable price. The better the atmosphere, the more maintenance members we will have. This is Lady USA's largest market and most likely to be our biggest consumers of daycare.

Group-X junkie

There are always those women who do not enjoy training by themselves and would prefer being in a group. They like the energy of group-x classes with the bumping music and the feeling of being in a crowd all working at the same pace. Group-X junkies are excellent at referring new members as it's easier to invite a friend to try out a new class than it is to talk them into coming to workout on the floor. Group-X junkies often run in pairs, sometimes in families (mother/daughter). Bargain offers such as "buy 3 get one 1 free" or "bring a friend for half price" promotions are excellent promotional tools for this segment.

Silver citizens

Silvers definitely prefer an all-women health club. Silvers are becoming increasingly aware of the benefits of a regular exercise program and more are participating now than ever before. When provided a health promoting program, senior citizens are willing to participate due to the new focus on physical activity in the elder years and constant encouragement from family and physicians. Silvers are budget conscious and somewhat nervous about trying machines and weights on their own. They are aware of the benefits but lack the knowledge about how to exercise safely and effectively. For this reason they are excellent candidates for personal training services. They also don't mind working out in small-groups and often actually view the health club as a possible extension of their social network.

For these reasons the silver segment should receive discounts that take into account the fact that many are no longer in the work force and may be living on a fixed income. Special membership discounts will be available for those 55 and over. Also, since silvers don't mind exercising in a small group and are often out of the workforce, its frequently the case that they can workout during normally slow times on the exercise floor. Special "55 and over" small group workout teams can be marketed and run mid-day, mid-week. Thus keeping the personal training staff busy with clients in the typically slow 10:00am – 3:00pm window.

4.2 Target Segment Strategy

Due to the size and convenient location of our facility many will be attracted to Lady USA and come inside to see what we have to offer, simply because they drive past everyday. However, we will not be content to wait for the customers to come to us. Instead, we will focus our marketing strategies on those market segments that match our offerings.

Our main objective with early marketing strategy will be to get women into the facility for a tour. Once women see what we have to offer, experience the décor and atmosphere, we feel confident they will want to return and participate in some of the many activities and programs that are available.

Some of the ways Lady USA will attract women into the facility include:

*Offering tours during the building an early completion stage of the facility.

*Having a large promotional "Grand Opening" event that will be catered and feature much fanfare.

*Hosting and sponsoring community events such as art shows, fun runs, etc.

*Mailer offers for free one-week passes to Castle Rock and the surrounding areas.

*Print and radio media promotions.

*A possible live remote broadcast with a local radio station.

*Co-marketing partnership with several local lady's apparel stores and boutiques.

*Co-marketing partnership with "The Daily Grind", a coffee and tea house less than one mile away.

4.3 Service Business Analysis

The sports and fitness business is a booming industry with total revenues of over $10.6 billion in 2006. As a result fitness clubs are opening all over the country, including such novel locations as airports and grocery stores. The size an scope of these clubs vary from small, individually owned workout studios to very elaborate, publicity owned franchises. In July 2007 there were 18,997 health clubs in the USA with over 30 million total members. That's an average of over 1,800 members per club. Multi-sport clubs like Lady USA averaged just over 2,800 members per club. One of Lady USA's challenges is to establish itself as a legitimate sports and fitness club that is appealing to each of its market segments and position itself as a great value for members and casual walk-ins alike.

4.4 Competition

While there is no direct competition for Lady USA in Castle Rock, two other clubs (Lady America and Curves) have locations less than 30 minutes away. These clubs do not incorporate a spa, tanning beds or an upgraded training program on a regular basis. Their exercise programs are based on the 30-minute circuit model, meaning individual members are not working on personalized programs designed to achieve specific goals. Rather, all members come in and go through the exact same routine. There are no personal trainers, neither offers daycare and hours are more limited than Lady USA.

Various types of memberships are available at each location although Lady of America does not offer paid-in-full memberships. The Curves studio is small and can only accommodate 12 patrons at a time.

5.0 Strategy Implementation Ideas

With virtually no competition in town, a current population of 65,000 and steadily growing, Lady USA has a very large potential market. Because of the small number of recreation and fitness facilities in Castle Rock (none catering to women only), we feel we will reach financial viability very quickly. This will be accomplished by actively and continuously promoting Lady USA through radio and media advertisements, a massive "Grand Opening" promotion, by hosting and supporting community events and entering into key strategic alliances with local businesses.

5.1 Competitive Edge

Lady USA has a two fold competitive edge. First, we will be the only full service salon and all-women's health an fitness club in the immediate geographic area. In addition, the scope and variety of programs run at the facility will be unmatched by any other club in the area. We also have superior location, size and appearance of the facility.

By maintaining our focus on our marketing strategy, program development and fulfillment, Lady USA will be known as the top full service salon and all-woman's health and fitness facility in Castle Rock and the south-Denver metro region.

However, our competitive edge may be diluted if we become complacent in program development and implementation. It will be important for us to keep up with the current trends in both sport and fitness programming.

To further establish a competitive edge, Lady USA will be a registered member of the International Physical Fitness Association (IPFA). In 2007 there were over 3,104 participating health clubs nationally. A major benefit to members is the IFPA All Clubs Unite program which states that if a member moves within a 25 mile radius of an IPFA affiliate, she may transfer her membership over to the club in the new location. If there is no IPFA facility in the new community the member may cancel her membership for a $50 cancellation fee, but then have no further commits to their remaining contract. This IFPA affiliation provide assurance and peace of mind to the members and will be another Lady USA exclusive for our community.

5.2 Sales Strategy

Sales in the sports and fitness industry are based on the type and quality of services and amenities provided by the facility. The "something for everyone" slogan fits perfectly with Lady USA. All users of our facility must feel like they are getting the best possible value and programs available for their money.

Prior to purchasing a membership each prospective new members will have the opportunity to meet with a representative and be educated on all membership options. During this discussion, the prospective member will be informed of all services, programs and available amenities. Our priority at this time is first to establish a relationship of trust with the prospective new member, second to sell a membership. Our sales staff must be trained and fully capable of not only sales, but of fostering relationships.

5.3 Sales Forecast

Chart 5.1 provides forecasted sales for regular memberships (it does not take into account discounted senior memberships or other odd-priced specials), add-ons, personal training and additional profit centers.

Chart 5.0

Regular Memberships		Monthly Average	
Year 1	**Two sales per day**	**Work days**	**Monthly totals**
Paid in full	$798	25	$19,950
Monthly	$59.90	25	$1,497.50
Enrollment Fee ($20)	$40	25	$1,000
Monthly Enrollment Fee ($40)	$80	25	$2,000
Annual Totals			$24,447.50
Yearly Totals			$293,370

Year 2	Three sales per day	Work days	Monthly totals
Paid in full	$1,197	25	$29,925
Monthly	$89.95	25	$2,246.25
Enrollment Fee ($20)	$60	25	$1,500
Monthly Enrollment Fee ($40)	$120	25	$3,000
Annual Totals			$36,671.25
Yearly Totals			$440,055
Year 3	Four sales per day	Work days	Monthly totals
Paid in full	$1,596	25	$39,900
Monthly	$119.80	25	$2,995
Enrollment Fee ($20)	$80	25	$2,000
Monthly Enrollment Fee ($40)	$160	25	$4,000
Annual Totals			$48,895
Yearly Totals			$586,740

* Note, the enrollment fee is comission paid to the sales rep on the sale. At this point, it is not added into the club's monthly projections but will be on our books.

Add-Ons   Monthly Average

Years 1-3	Two sales per day	Work days	Monthly totals
Tanning (paid in full)	$298	25	$7,450
Tanning (monthly a-la-carte)	$39.90	25	$997.50
Monthly totals			$8,447.50
Annual total			$101,370
Years 1-3	Two sales per day	Work days	Monthly totals
Daycare (paid in full)	$298	25	$7,450
Daycare (monthly a-la-carte)	$39.90	25	$997.50
Monthly totals			$8,447.50
Annual total			$101,370

Personal Training

Years 1-3	One sale per day
60% of $60 per hr.	$36
Yearly totals	

Monthly average

Work days	Monthly totals
35	$900
	$10,800

Additional Profit

Years 1-3	Booth rental per month	Monthly Totals
Hair	$500	$500
Nails	$500	$500
Massage	$500	$500
Cosmetics	$500	$500
Monthly totals		$2,000
Yearly totals		$24,000

Projected Totals (with out enrollment fees)

Year 1	Memberships	Add-ons	Booth rent	Personal training
Paid in full	$19,950	$14, 900	$2,000	$900
Monthly	$1,497.50		$1,995	
Total monthly receivable		$41,242		
Total annual receivable		$494,904		
Year 2	Memberships	Add-ons	Booth rent	Personal training
Paid in full	$29,925	$14,900	$2,000	$900
Monthly	$2,246.25		$1,995	
Total monthly receivable		$51,966		
Total annual receivable		$51,966		
Year 2	Memberships	Add-ons	Booth rent	Personal training
Paid in full	$39,900	$14,900	$2,000	$900
Monthly	$2,995		$1,995	
Total monthly receivable		$62,690		
Total annual receivable		$752,280		

5.3 Milestone Schedule

The accompanying table lists important program milestones, with dates, managers in charge and budgets for each. The milestone schedule indicates our emphasis on planning for implementation. What the table doesn't show is the commitment behind it. Our business plan includes complete provisions for plan-vs.-actual analysis, and we will hold monthly follow-up meetings to discuss the variance, course directions and corrections if needed.

Milestone	Start Date	End Date	Budget
Business Plan	05/01/20xx	12/01/20xx	$0
Concept Plan Reveiw	06/01/20xx	08/08/20xx	$0
Financial Backing Presentation	07/15/20xx	08/08/20xx	$0
Company set up	09/18/20xx	11/18/20xx	$15,000
Logo Design	10/01/20xx	11/01/20xx	$0
Other			$0

Total $15,000

6.0 Management Summary

The initial management team for Lady USA depends mainly on the Julie Barger. Julie will stay with in her expertise in running the day-to-day operations of the facility such as scheduling, marketing and promotions, as well as developing community programs. Back up includes staff members who will compliment Julie and bring experience in other areas. For example, qualified personnel will be hired for hair, nails and massage. General staff will be hired on an as-needed basis as the number of women using the facility increases. There will also be custodial services and maintenance of the facility which will fall under the general manager (Julie's) responsibilities.

6.1 Personnel Plan

Table 6.0 provides a schedule of Lady USA personnel and compensation.

Projected Compensation

Employee	Year 1	Year 2	Year 3
General Manager	$50,000	$53,000	$55,000
Office Manager	$25,000	$28,000	$30,000
Training Manager	$0	$36,000	$37,000
General Staff	$80,448	$85,448	$87,000
Custodial	$10,296	$12,238	$13,714
Total Payroll	**$165,744**	**$214,686**	**$222,714**
Total # employees	15	17	18

Table 6.1 provides a projected employee schedule. (These are schedules will not be used immediately but once company is established.)

Employee Schedule

Employee	Mon.	Tues.	Wed.	Thurs.	Fri.	Sat.
General Mgr.	9-7	9-7	9-7	9-7	9-7	9-1
Sales A	9-9	-	9-9	-	9-8	-
Sales B	-	9-9	-	9-9	-	8-3
Sales C	7-1	7-1	7-1	7-1	7-1	-
Sales D	4-9	4-9	4-9	4-9	4-8	-
Personal Trainer 1	4-9	4-9	4-9	4-9	4-8	9-1
Personal Trainer 2	9-1	9-1	9-1	9-1	-	-

Total Hours: 124

*124 hrs. per wk. x $6 per hr. x 4 wks.= **$3,048 per month payable**
*Owner is not included in hourly. This is a salary, previously listed.

*Personal trainers are not listed in payables as they earn a 60/40 split with club.

Daycare

Employeee	Mon.	Tues.	Wed.	Thurs.	Fri.	Sat.
A.	8-4	8-4	8-4	8-4	8-4	-
B.	10-1	10-1	10-1	10-1	10-1	8-11
C.	4-9	4-9	4-9	4-9	4-8	8-3
D.	5-7	5-7	5-7	5-7	5-7	-

Total Hours: 99

* 99 hrs. per wk. at $6 per hour, 4 wks. = **$2,376 per month payable**

Group-X Classes

Employee	Mon.	Tues.	Wed.	Thurs.	Fri.	Sat.
7 am	kickbox		step	spin	yoga	tone
8 am	combo					
10 am	pilates	tone	pilates	tone	pilates	pilates
12 pm	aerobics	hip hop	aerobics	hip hop	yoga	yoga
1 pm	-	-	-	-	-	Kids
5 pm	combo	yoga	tone	step	aerobics	
6 pm	hip hop	salsa	hip hop	-	salsa	hip hop
7 pm	yoga	yoga	-	yoga	-	-

Total Hours: 32

* 32 hrs. per wk x $10 per class x 4 wks. = **$1,280 per month payable**

7.0 Financial Plan

Lady USA will require an initial investment (start up) amount of approximately $135,000. This funding will be coming from a combination of a private investor (30%) and a small business loan (70%) from Vectra Bank of Colorado Springs, Colorado. Combined monthly loan payments will be approximately $10,000 with the private investor not requiring any interest on his loan and imposing a five year payback horizon. The Vectra Bank loan will carry interest in the amount of the prime interest rate plus one and a half percent. Payments to both parties are to be made on or by the fifth day of each month with Vectra

Bank imposing a $39 penalty for any payments made after the 15th of the month.

7.1 Important Assumptions

The financial plan depends on important assumptions. The monthly assumptions are included in the appendices. From the beginning, we recognize that collection days are critical, but not a factor we can influence easily. At least we are planning on the problem and dealing with it. Interest rate, tax rates and personal burden are based on conservative assumptions.

Some of the more important underlying assumptions are: we assume a strong economy, without major recession, we assume the rate of growth in the fitness industry will continue along its current path.

7.2 Break-even Analysis

This analysis is base solely on membership sales with no regard to the income generated by daily walk-in fees, pro shop or hair, nail and massage revenue. With our fixed costs of approximately $53,000 at the onset, we need to sell an average of 82 memberships per month to effectively break even from year one operations.

7.3 Projected Profit and Loss

Profit and loss is shown on the following table. We show a conservative estimate of 7% - 8% of net profit/sales, with that number increasing by approximately 7% per year. According to the research done through the last 12 years of my career, these projections are very conservative and should easily be obtained.

Table 7.0 – Profit/Loss Statement

	Year 1	Year 2	Year 3
Sales	$530,892	$677,580	$824,268
Direct cost of sales	$0	$0	$0
Production payroll	$0	$0	$0
Other	$0	$0	$0
Equipment lease	$36,000	$36,000	$36,000
Loan payment	$10,000	$10,000	$10,000
Total cost of sales	$0	$0	$0
Gross margin	$530,892	$677,580	$824,268
Gross margin %	100%	100%	100%
Expenses:			
Payroll	$162,000	$207,750	$217,538
Sales and Marketing	#30,000	$30,000	$30,000
Depreciation	$0	$0	$0
Telephone	$6,000	$6,000	$6,000
Utilites	$18,000	$18,000	$18,000
Insurance	$12,000	$12,600	$13,230
Payroll Taxes	$38,149	$47,937	$50,003
Rent	$108,000	$108,000	$108,000
Total Operating Expenses	$420,149	$476,287	$488,771
Gross profit	$110,743	$201,293	$335,497
Interest Expense			
Taxes incurred	$11,586	$25,921	$49,335
Net profit	**$99,157**	**$99,157**	**$286,162**

7.4 Projected Cash Flow (to be completed once open for business)

Lady USA is being built in Castle Rock. This location is a build suit site, which is due for completion in January 20xx. I plan on contracting pre sales out of a business trailer while the club is being built. This will generate a minimum of $50,000 prior to opening. This revenue figure is based on selling two memberships per day with tanning and daycare. This is a conservative figure since approximately 75% of members will require daycare. At an average membership cost of $299 x 2 sales per day people = $598 in sales per day, x 75 working days until opening = $44,850 gross sales revenue.

In addition, daycare sales generate $11,495 (based on pre-opening special of $65 for three months of unlimited child care to 209 members which is 75% of initial sales) in gross sales to this same group and a tanning upgrade generates another $2,242 (based on 25% of initial sales purchasing a $29.99 3-month unlimited special). Assuming 100% of new members pay with cash or credit (that is, they do not become a distant account receivable) the total pre-sale revenue should come to $58,587.

Lady USA will have several memberships to choose from. We will offer 3 to 36 month memberships. Prior to opening all memberships will be offered on a discounted basis. Upon opening our price will continue at the discounted advertised rate for a "Grand Opening Weekend" special promotion, before reverting to regular rates. Pre-sales and grand opening rates will be:

    3-month membership = $149
    6-month membership = $199
    12-month membership = $299
    24-month membership = $399
    36-month membership = $499

We will also have month-to-month memberships available at a rate of $54.95 per month. Tanning and daycare are an additional $19.95 each per month for all membership levels. Daycare or tanning may be pre-paid for one full year for $149 each.

Monthly payments will be auto-deducted from the members' checking, savings or credit card account. American Service financing will be our merchant services finance company and will take care of all of our membership billing.

Additional services such as massage, hair, nails and cosmetic procedures (collagen, botox, facials, chemical peels, etc.) will be priced and sold a-la-cart by the independent contractor providing the service. Contractors will rent booths for a flat rate of $500 per month from each renter and may price their products and services independently but with my supervision and approval.

Taking a look at the fast growing pace of Castle Rock and based on my past experience I forecast that three months into the business Lady USA's total income should be approximately $50,000 - $90,000. This is consistent with health clubs I have managed past last fifteen years. Again, based on prior experience and knowledge or typical membership sales fluctuations, I forecast the following monthly income.

January	$87,000
February	$84,000
March	$88,000
April	$81,000
May	$61,000
June	$53,000
July	$47,000
August	$43,000
September	$46,000
October	$48,000
November	$45,000
December	$37,000

This is an estimated yearly gross of $720,000 receivable cash. Assuming the club, being a new facility, gets off to a slow start and generates less-than-average sales revenues it's first year.

January	$50,000
February	$50,000
March	$50,000
April	$50,000
May	$45,000
June	$45,000
July	$40,000
August	$35,000
September	$35,000
October	$30,000
November	$30,000
December	$30,000

This is an estimated $490,000 annual gross with $327,000 in payables, plus $24,000 in booth rentals equals a yearly profit of $187,000. Our accounting records will be kept on a daily basis with a day sheet.

7.5 Detailed Cash Flow Analysis (to be completed once open for business)

Cash flow projections show annual amounts only. Cash flow projections are critical to our success. The annual cash flow projections included here are to be completed once flow can be monitored. Detailed monthly numbers are to be kept and reviewed by the General Manager and Office Managers weekly for the first full year of operation.

Cash Flow Analysis

Cash Flow In
Cash from operations
    Cash from membership sales
    Cash from monthly dues
    Cash from receivables
        Proshop sales
        Contractor rents received
        Misc.
Subtotal Cash from Operations
Additional cash received

Non-operating Income
Sales tax
VAT, HST/GST received
New (current) borrowing
New other liabilities (interest free)
New long-term liabilities
Sales of current assets
Sales of long-term assets
New investment received
Subtotal cash received

Cash Flow Out
Expenditures from operations
Cash spending
Payment of account payable
Subtotal spent on operations

Additional cash spent
Non operating expense
Sales tax
VAT/HST/GST paid out
Principal repayment or current borrowing
Other liabilities principal repayment
Long-term liabilities principal repayment
Purchases, other current assets

Purchases, long-term assets
Dividends paid
Subtotal cash spent
Net cash flow
Cash Balance

7.6 Projected Balance sheet

The balance sheet in the following table shows managed but sufficient growth of net worth, and a sufficiently healthy financial position.

Balance sheet
Assets
Current assets
Cash
Account receivable
Inventory
Other current assets
Total current assets
Long term assets
Accumulated depreciation
Total long term assets
Total Assets

Liabilities
Accounts payable
Current borrowing
Other current liabilities
Subtotal current liabilities
Long-term liabilities
Total liabilities
Paid-in capital
Retained earnings
Total capital
Total liabilities and capital

Net worth

Appendix

In most cases when developing a business plan these accounting forms are necessary to properly organize the business. Attach them to the business plan. These forms are available, can be found, downloaded and put into use from any number of accounting forms sites on the internet.

Comparing the two business plans

At this point the major difference between the two business plans and models (mobile training versus an actual health club) should be readily apparent, but just in case you've missed it – *START-UP COST*. The mobile training business is one with a start-up amount that's a fraction of a gym, practically no on-going over-head expenses, little or no payroll, facility and equipment leases, janitorial expenses, etc. It has the capability of making just as much money as owning a health club does when viewed from a net/net basis. While a person may not make as much gross income, practically 100% of his or her income stays in his pocket. As opposed to small business loans, lease payments and everything else involved in keeping the doors to a club open.

As you are developing your business plan make sure to compare the major differences in the two plans. We have seen gym business plans requiring as much as a $22 million dollar initial investment. A more typical start-up amount for a modest sized gym is something in the $250,000 range for a gym and about $100,000 for a studio.

When examining investment amounts in isolation there is no comparison between the two. A mobile fitness company can literally be started with $500. The difference is flexibility and risk. In the early years the typical gym owner has no flexibility. For the most part, if the doors are open, she has to be there.

The hours are incredibly long. And of course anytime you're borrowing hundreds of thousands of dollars, or investing hundreds of thousands of your own money, risk is inherent.

A brief note on time management

Before diving head first into the business plan waters, we want to insert a quick sidebar concerning time management. We always get out of our business what we put into it. That's unavoidable. Effective time management is one of the most important factors in getting any business launched. We've seen great managers fail as independent business owners, in some cases quite quickly, because they had poor time management skills. Before beginning to implement the business plan, learn how to manage time.

Why is time management so important?

A huge part of developing a business plan is setting a schedule to manage time effectively. It's a necessary prerequisite for anyone interested in running a successful company. Strict time management analysis and plans should be in place for you as the owner, and then implemented for anyone you hire as you grow. Time management is also part of obtaining goals. You need to use time properly so you do not start making excuses which tend to be directed towards failure. Understand that managing time effectively and teaching employees to do the same makes both of you accountable for activity.

We suggest adopting a time management schedule. A quality time management schedule allows you to direct efforts towards the vision and business plan rather than just doing what you can in a determined amount of time.

Use of a time management chart

We use the chart below on a daily basis for managing time. Over the years we've learned that failure to follow a set hour to hour plan leads easily to side tracking and a failure to accomplish daily goals. Failure to accomplish daily goals leads to failure to accomplish weekly ones. Which leads to monthly; which leads to annual; which leads to going out of business. Every day needs structure.

Your daily schedule will be determined by your vision and business plan. First, you will take a look at your business plan and vision and allocate the time necessary to work on each task, developing and as you grow, hire and add other business functions.

Documentation equals organization

For some people time management can be as simple as documenting their schedule and goals and placing them someplace they will be seen every day. Upon reading this section one of our partners commented, "I began developing a business outline of what I was going to accomplish on a weekly basis and my productivity increased probably 50% overnight. When I was able to check off tasks at the end of the week it allowed me to better organize my thoughts." Simply writing businesses goals and tasks out for each week can easily make you much more productive.

Accountability

This all goes back to keeping yourself and your business accountable on a daily basis. The chart below allows you to make a time management schedule and check off the given box when tasks are complete. Being accountable for actions (or inactions) is one of the most important things you can ever do. Effectively manage time and you become accountable for it on a daily basis.

Incorporating Personal Time

A lot of new business owners do not account for personal time. It's very important to schedule and hour for lunch, time with family or kids. Believe it or not this is just as important to your business as working is. If you become frustrated because you don't have enough time, sit back and determine how to fix it. This is important. If you find yourself frustrated or aggravated with the business your productivity will start to slip.

Chart 7.0 - Daily Time Management

Time	Event	Complete
5-6	Train Amy Wescott	X
6-7	Train Tim Wescott	X
8-9	Develop internet marketing system	X
10-11	Develop internet marketing system	X
11-12	Visit ABC equipment store and bring flyers	X
12-1	Lunch	X
1-2	Visit Vitamin Store and ABC Condos with business packets	X
3-4	Return emails and submit on Craig's list and 25 other web lists	X
5-6	Create my hiring packet to hire new trainers and make tomorrows time management schedule.	X
7-8	Family Time	
9-10	Family Time	

*A sample Daily Time Management sheet is available in the appendix. Use it for your own purposes to maintain control of each and every day.

Building a Better Business Plan

What you have seen thus far is the framework needed to construct a quality business plan. And a quality business plan is a must. Those who begin business without one are starting off behind the eight ball. In following the VGB system mentioned in chapter one you now have developed a business vision and goals. Now its time to take both the vision and goals and turn them into a structured business plan. Do this by inputting your vision and goals into the business plan example that has been provided. It may not be perfect and you may not be able to fill in each and every section at first. That's ok, the critical thinking this process stimulates is invaluable. The mobile fitness training plan in this book is easy to follow and organize. It will provide structure, a skeleton, so to speak. You can fill in the muscles as you go.

So stop here. If you have not already, develop your vision and goals, and then begin the process of starting the actual business plan. You're 70% of the way there, now it's time to take ideas and commit them to paper. Its time to turn your business vision and goals into a business plan!

Chapter Four

Business Plan Implementation

It is now time to start implementing the VGB system and developing business. Your business is now ready to open and you should have the final business plan in your hands! The VGB system is in place and now you start working on growing the business.

Business Plan Implementation

"Great, where do I get started?" Now that you've developed your business plan it is time to start learning how to implement it. Do this through learning different organization, marketing, advertising, networking, vendor and other successful systems. We have worked as mobile fitness professionals for years and now operate a very successful business. We've gone through the trial and error process and one of the goals of this book is to help you avoid some of our mistakes. We are now going to help you implement your business and start making some money!

Throughout these next sections we are going to provide systems and ideas for you to start developing business. Developing business in our industry is based mostly upon developing relationships. We have a very strong vendor system for you to learn, master this and marketing plans along with other ideas will flow forth from it.

Once you have your VGB system its time to target your market. Keep in mind this is the same market whether you own health club or a mobile training business. It is all about building relationships with people and businesses in the community.

Marketing and promoting

The first book of *"The Success Express"* series, titled *"90-Days to a FULL Client Base"* devotes an entire chapter to the "5 P's" of marketing (price, place, product, people, promotion). We highly recommend picking up a copy as it's unnecessarily redundant to repeat all of the information here. Please forgive this shameless plug, but the chapter does cover some very important aspects of marketing in great detail and with real life examples.

The secrets to becoming successful fall within your ability to market and promote your business effectively. If you are not willing to get out and pound the pavement you will not develop the relationships necessary for the business to grow and generate clients. There is no replacement for hard work.

Developing strategic alliances

The age old saying, "It's not what you know it's who you know" is only two thirds correct. To be completely accurate this saying should read, "It's not what you know it's who you know, *then* it's what you know." This difference is slight but important. Having excellent relationships in place with key vendors (businesses capable of generating clients) is the most important aspect of the growth phase. You must begin to develop a strategy of locating and entering into mutually beneficial relationships with other businesses in the community. In the "Secrets to Success" section of this book we will explore how to find and develop the relationships to implement these alliances.

Networking and developing vendors for your mobile training company and is one of the most important and time consuming jobs you have. Your job is to develop relationships with other professionals and businesses in your region that can help provide you business. A quality networking partner just does not help provide you business but they help provide a network of business owners that you can refer as well making your business stronger.

What is networking?

Networking is and will always be one of the most important things any business owner can do. Networking should be done on a daily and consistent basis. Networking is developing relationships with other professionals or any entity who is able to refer or provide you business and for whom you can do the same.

You could network with a physical therapist, a vitamin store, other personal trainers, or even your local Taco Bell. As a business owner your networking skills need to become sharp and organized. You need to understand that almost every person or business in the world has something to offer you.

What is a vendor?

Vendors are simply your networking partners. A vendor can be a company or a person that is able to send you business or provide a professional service for your company. Don't under estimate or under utilize your vendors. Take a second and ask yourself how could a Taco Bell really benefit your business? Of course the neighborhood Taco Bell would not be particularly high on the target list, but it's manager could be a potential networking partner never the less. Ever walked into a fast food place, a juice stop or such a location and seen your local gym has a drop box for business cards and a free week of training? That's nothing but creative marketing. By developing the relationship with the local Taco Bell they ended up with a drop box that's probably generating 150 new member leads a month. That box probably cost the gym four dollars, if they gain just one client a year out of it, how's that for a rate of return? Your goal is to get in front of the public eye and having networking partners that will provide such opportunities helps to brand your business name in the area.

Referring networking partners

Referring networking partners is also very important. Nobody likes relationships that are the equivalent of a one-way street. Never be labeled as just in the business of trying to get but not give. People talk and word travels fast. Be in the business of providing leads as well. You won't always be able to refer partners as much as they can you and vice versa. But strive to maintain somewhat of a balance.

There is nothing necessarily wrong with compensating networking partners for referrals, but it falls into one of those vague, "be careful" areas. Some partners will jump at the opportunity, others may find it unprofessional at best, rude at worst. If not outright compensation a nice token gift and/or greeting card expressing appreciation is usually a safe way to go.

Prepare for the vendor meetings

Before going out to meet with a prospective vendor—be prepared. This includes having all your company literature organized, neatly bound and ready to be reviewed, a stack of business cards to leave behind and always be well groomed and dressed. There's never a second chance to make a first impression, make the one you want to leave behind forever.

Discuss your business and where its going and don't be afraid to talk vision. People like and are generally impressed by forward thinkers. Discuss what you have to offer and any areas of expertise you may posses. Always make an effort to get the prospective partner talking about their background, education, family, etc. People enjoy discussing themselves, especially proud business owners. Its been said that God gave us two ears and one mouth for a reason, that we might listen twice as much as we speak — an excellent proverb to live by.

While listening be constantly asking the question "How can I benefit this person?" Demonstrate that you're not just here to obtain business but to develop a relationship that benefits all. This is a very important trait you must master. The value of strong partners cannot be overstated, nor can the graveness of having poor ones or worse yet, having none.

Places and people to network with

It goes without saying that some businesses are likely to be poor partners and some complete wastes of time. Having a strong relationship with a funeral parlor is probably of little use. Most of their clients are lacking adequate flexibility and stamina (a resting heart rate of zero beats per minute isn't particularly promising) to begin working with you and family members are simply not in a frame of mind for Joe Funeral Director to hand over one of your business cards and say, "This gal does great work." However an individual with a health food multi-level business may be a great source. See List 3.0 for a list of places we have had excellent success with as business vendors.

Using the phone book, internet and good old fashioned neighborhood canvassing develop your own list and then just jump in head first. On a daily basis, systematically begin to set up appointments get out and market yourself and your company Go through the complete vendor system below, develop goals and stick to them.

List 3.0

Some quality places to network with for finding mobile training clients. We have had tremendous success with some of these vendors and have dedicated sections later in this book on marketing to this specific business

Fitness equipment stores
Sporting good stores
Vitamin/nutrition/health foods stores
Golf shops
Pro shops
Physical therapists
Medical doctors
Chiropractors
Nutritionists
Health care providers
Senior centers
Residential communities with fitness centers (condos, town homes, apartments, assisted living centers, etc.)
Support groups
Leads groups
Beauty salons
Other fitness professionals (who do not provide mobile services)
Schools
Newspapers

Social gatherings (Chamber of Commerce mixers, etc.) Consistency is one of the keys to having a successful vendor system. Have a non-stop attitude toward becoming a successful networker. Dress for success and introduce yourself to everyone! Set a goal to schedule least five meetings each week with prospective partners then work like crazy to make it happen. Your vendor and networking system is not a product of luck. It will happen and grow as the result of consistent effort to market yourself and your business.

Vendor and Networking Program

We are going to now start developing your vendor program. This program is going to provide structure in pursuit of vendors and business partners. Many trainers and business owners have tried to develop such systems but few have consistently made it work. Our goal is to outline your vendor system and develop a plan directed towards landing strategic partners— the more the merrier.

Begin by creating two very important lists using the forms in the appendix. The professional contacts list should be a list of 50 individuals such as massage therapists, physical therapists, etc. who can benefit your business with a networking relationship. The businesses contacts list can be a sandwich or deli shop, window cleaners, or perhaps an auto repair shop. These are business locations you can advertise at and partner with, not necessarily a professional with his or her own client base.

Identify and use these forms to list 100 prospective vendors in your area. Then begin this step-by-step process:

Step 1

Take the lists form in the appendix identify and complete each with no fewer than 50 potential vendors from your area you anticipate providing fitness services to. Use the list of possible networking sources (also found in the appendix) on to help you organize your thoughts.

Step 2

Spend one day contacting all 100 prospective vendors on the lists. In many cases you will get voice mail, answering machines, secretaries or assistants and not be able to through to the actual individual with whom you would like to meet. This is unavoidable. Leave a polite message, at the very least you are a bug in their ear and making them aware you're on the block. When/if you do get through to the person the goal is to schedule a face-to-face meeting. Spend a brief amount of time explaining what your company has to offer, then ask when would be a convenient time to meet *at their place of business.* If they ask questions simply let them know you are interested in the possibility of developing a networking relationship.

In some cases you may be asked to send information before a meeting is agreed to. When this happens kindly agree and provide a single page personalized information letter on you and your business. Staple a business card to it and drop it in the mail <u>the same day</u>. Promptness is a quality all professionals appreciate. The letter should be brief, explain what you have to offer and what you are trying to accomplish.

Should you successfully schedule the meeting right there on the phone chances are good you have hit the jackpot. That is, you have found someone who understands the value of networking partnerships, they are interested in business and have swung the door open wide. All you have to do is make sure you are prepared for the meeting and make a positive impression.

Step 3

Beginning the week after initial contacts begin to re-contact all prospective vendors on a weekly basis until you either get a meeting or get a "no, we are not interested". Being afraid of rejection had been the death of more than one salesman. No doesn't mean they are not interested, it just means they aren't interested at this time. Keep them on your list and re-contact them later. Often times the persistence is what ultimately leads to the prospect agreeing to meet.

Step 4

Set a weekly vendor goal. An excellent start is, "I will meet with five prospective vendors every week for two consecutive months. This goal, if hit, will result in a total of forty prospective vendor meetings. A plan like that is bound to result in a handful of power partners.

Of course you are going to have situations where prospective vendors on your list are just not panning out and you need to delete them. Don't spend all of your effort an energy digging in a dry well. If you've tried reaching them for weeks and have had no luck, drop them. If they told you "no thanks", transfer them to a wait and see list, add some new vendors to the current list and keep pushing. Always try to have 100 vendors on your lists to follow up and work on. This will give you ample prospects. Once a meeting has happened, transfer them onto an "Active vendor" and work on your marketing materials or whatever items were agreed to in the meeting. Remember, a bird in the hand is very valuable. Always act immediately to impress new partners.

When implementing the business plan always remember that developing vendors is one of the most important things you will do. Give this the effort it requires and you'll be well on the road to success. No matter how corny it may sound, signing a personal commitment to business activity works. Dig in on the previous four steps and you're bound to strike gold. An example of a personal commitment follows. Use this or create one of your own, but either way, having a commitment in writing is a critical step.

Personal Commitment

I agree to schedule _____ meetings every week to develop my networking and vendor relationships and each week will not cease working until this goal has been achieved.

Signed_____

Date_____

Active vendors

Any vendor who agrees to work with you can be reclassified as an active partner. You don't necessarily have to be getting business from them but you do have to be in contact with them and trying to develop business together. When a vendor becomes active, its time to begin building. Start by trying to develop strategies to obtain clients and business from them while at the same time developing cross-promotional campaigns wherein you can refer business back to them as well. Use a simple sheet like Chart 3.0 to keep track of active marketing activities with active vendors. Visit often and always be thinking creatively about ways to cross-market with vendors.

Consider the vendor and what they may have to offer. Are you likely to have clients in common? Do they have a retail or store front where you can place signage and/or other promotional materials? Do they maintain communication with their customer base via a newsletter, e-newsletter or mailers and if so, can you get an insert? If they do mailers, can you acquire the mailing list and send out a special offer? Placing mutual links on websites is another quick and easy exchange.

Once you've landed a new partner, stay in constant contact. Use e-mail, fax, text messages, phone conversations and drop in visits. Don't become a pest, but don't allow them to forget about you either. This is yet another area where a delicate balance must be reached. The goal is to develop a relationship, but not at the expense of being annoying. You want them to look forward to your email or call. There is no exact science but trust us, you'll get a feel for each individual's feelings and personally and be able to adjust accordingly. Remember, like yours, the partner's time is valuable. As a business owner they must view time spent with you as a benefit.

Chart 3.0

Ways vendor can provide you business	Ways you can provide vendor business	Notes

Organizing the active vendor list

Below is an example of an active vendor list and how to organize it. We recommend using an Excel spreadsheet for easy access and organization but we've seen business owners become successful using a pen and pad. The format doesn't matter. What matters is the organization and effort put into it.

Chart 3.1

Date	Vendor name & contact	Contact information	This weeks activity(s)

Unresponsive vendors

If a vendor suddenly becomes unresponsive, as will sometimes be the case, take an honest approach to the situation. As often as not they've simply gotten busy and paying attention to you isn't high on he priority list. Ask if they don't feel that the relationship is beneficial or if you did anything inappropriate. The partner will generally respond to your question and either start giving you more attention or disappear. If they disappear it probably means they wouldn't have worked very well anyway and you were quite likely wasting your time. Cut ties and move on.

Never give up on a vendor but put non-responsive ones on the back burning and focus on others. Come back and look at them again in the future. Marketing statistics have shown it may take getting in front of a customer as many as nine times before they are responsive to what you have to offer. This can be the same when dealing with vendors.

The #1 power partner

In our nearly forty combined years of experience running mobile fitness services companies we have discovered that there is one business in particular that has the potential to really put your business over the top. Fitness equipment retailers.

Partnering with equipment stores represents the ultimate win-win. The store gets an excellent sales feature—the ability to send a certified personal trainer right to customer's homes for a "free" in-home personal training session with the purchase of a piece of equipment. In turn, each time you go out and perform one of these complimentary sessions you are exposed to a potential new in-home client.

In exchange for a store agreeing to provide you their past-customers list you allow them to incorporate you into their sales and promotional literature ("Now providing in-home personal training!") , offer to provide a guaranteed session for every sale over $500, create a refer-back program to the store program whereby you are effectively up-selling the customer for them, thus increasing store sales totals.

Other excellent vendors

The following businesses have also proven to be winners when it comes to client referrals. We recommend finding each and every one of them within a 20-minute perimeter of the territory you intend to work and them make contacting them a high priority.

- Specialty fitness equipment stores (hiking and climbing, stores that sell higher end shoes for runners, outdoorsman stores, skate and surf, etc.)

- Sporting good stores or any location that sells fitness equipment. (Sporting goods stores can provide excellent client leads but are more difficult to get into relationship with as they are typically corporate-owned and do not have decision making autonomy at the local level. To go this route try developing relationships with specific members of the floor sales staff.)

Chapter Five

Opening the Client Relationship

Now that you have relationships in place in the local business community and are receiving a steady diet of new client inquiries and (ultimately) new clients, its time to begin the process of entering the prospective client's homes and developing a client base.

Much of this process is common sense and much of it is very similar to opening the vendor relationship. That is, be prompt, well groomed, dressed professionally (for our industry, of course) and demonstrate superior knowledge and confidence.

Consultations
We have found the best way to get the relationship rolling is by first scheduling an in-home consultation. When a prospective client contacts you about hiring you (or you contact them) the first thing you want to do is meet with prospect. This meeting has several goals, to find out where they live and determine if working with them makes sense given time and distance (if it doesn't then it's time to begin hiring trainers, but that's another discussion), discuss the prospect's goals, current health status, your rates and a host of other issues.

The question of charging for the consultation comes up frequently. In our Colorado businesses we do not charge for initial consultations. The thinking being a prospective client may get turned off at the prospect, go away and never become a client—possibly costing us thousands in future revenue. On the other hand, if we do the consultation for free and they prospect does become a client, that zero revenue hour will come back to us many times over the ensuing years, both from the client and referrals he or she provides.

What ever your decision have everything outlined and stick to the pattern. Should you decide to offer a complimentary consultation make sure not to call it "free". The word free tends to devalue things. Always choose "complimentary" or "no charge" or some other term.

Prior to scheduling the consultation many mobile fitness business owners will ask for a credit card to hold the prospect's spot. This provides protection against no-shows. You may tell the prospect the session is complimentary, so long as they show up, but if they do not they will be charged $50 or whatever the going rate in the area is. While some prospects may balk at the maneuver, most will recognize this is just good business on your part and it may even win the respect of some.

The consultation process
It's important to have a rehearsed, systematic method for performing consultations. You cannot afford to lose prospect as close to becoming a client as this. The following process has worked well for us over the years

Phone call (first contact)
Getting introduced is the first order of business with a new prospect. The first thing out of your mouth will set the mood for the entire conversation—so make it good. A polite greeting that should be precise and lead directly into the rest of the conversation is always best. There's no need to stick to a script but something along these lines is perfectly fine, "Hello may I speak with Sandy, please? Hi Sandy, this is Darrell calling with

Supreme Fitness, I understand you're interested in personal training, do you have a few moments to talk?"

Polite, simple, to the point. There will be time for chitchat and small talk soon enough, for the moment respect the prospects time and be direct without being curt. Set up a time to come to the prospect's home and perform the consultation. On the initial call find out what equipment, if any, the prospect has in their home. If possible, get specific the make and model of everything so you can research the piece(s) and become an expert on their home gym equipment.

Personal history (initial face-to-face meeting)
Without prying or getting personal try to obtain as much information about the client as possible. Discuss her fitness background. Determine what exercise she's doing, if any, how often, how long and how much. Get information on all parts of her fitness program; cardio, muscle conditioning and flexibility. Discuss nutrition, injury status, sleeping habits and stress levels. Listen for key pieces of information. Is she a beginner? Is there an injury you can help rehabilitate? Is she neglecting key fitness components that you can address? Ask a lot of questions and take notes on the answers. People love to talk about themselves. If you let them do so they will leave their interaction with a favorable impression of you.

Goals
Of course discovering exactly why the client wants to work with you is incredibly important. Is it weight loss for a specific event in 3 months that she needs to fit into a dress for? Is he hoping to run a 5k this summer? Or just general conditioning? Be sure to probe so you are very clear about expectations. Always talk about goals!

Comments, questions and conversation around the following sentences are always productive:

- What specific changes are you looking for?
- In what ways would your life be better?
- How often will you be exercising?
- Have you discussed this with your wife/husband?
- Bring up a exercise evaluation and what it details
- What works best, personal training, nutrition counseling or both?

Action Plan

Here's where you get to explain how you can help. Be sure to relate everything you say back to items the prospect shared concerning goals Focus on the benefits, not the features of your program. Improved cardiovascular function is a feature. You'll be able to keep up with your twin 6-year old grand daughters when they visit and want to go for walk is a benefit. Learn how to decipher the difference.

Share the plan with the prospect and now discuss frequency of sessions, duration of sessions and your rates. Be sure to have a professional rate sheet or card that you have developed. Place on the table and go over it thoroughly with the prospect. When it comes billing time, surprises are always a bad thing.

Conclusion

Book the first appointment, which is typically an evaluation or assessment session. Determine whether you will perform a basic or comprehensive fitness assessment. Tell her what she can expect during the first session. Ask her to pick up, fill out and return the client questionnaire, health history form, waiver of liability, medical clearance and/or what ever documentation you require new clients to complete.

Thank the client
Presumably, hopefully, this step is self-explanatory.

Demonstration sessions
Since we spent so much time in the previous chapter discussing the merits of partnering with fitness equipment retailers, we thought it important to outline the content of a demonstration session, or "demos". To differentiate a demo from a consultation, the demo is the in-home session that the store uses as a closing tool for selling equipment to clients. We have successfully leveraged the demonstration session into a very handsome annual revenue figure and its importance cannot be overstated. Should you succeed in landing a partnership with an equipment retailer, the information contained in the following sections will be invaluable.

One of the most important things to realize is that the purpose of the demo is not to place the prospect on an exercise program — that's what your services are for — but rather to explain how to properly and safely use their new piece of equipment. Proper seat height adjustment, safe execution of certain movements, etc. A demo session is a demonstration of how to use their equipment, nothing more nothing less. The session does not include an exercise prescription.

As with the consultation, its important to lay out a process for demonstration sessions. Below is the process we employ in the Colorado market and think is as good as any.

Initial phone call

"Hello is Helen available? Hello Helen, this is Stacey with Achieve Fitness USA. We're the firm that provides the complimentary in-home personal training session that was included with the purchase of your home gym last week, has (the store name) delivered and set it up yet? Great."

Build a little rapport and let them know that the reason for your call is to set up their complimentary in-home session. Be sure to get the following information; address, best phone number to contact them, age, any medical or other concerns that you should be made aware of, goals, specific piece(s) of equipment they purchased.

"Excellent, what would be an ideal time this week for me to come by and show you how the (equipment name) can help you achieve your fitness goals?"

Often times when making the demo setup call you will get a voice mail. Simply leave a polite message that is short and to the point. "Hello, this message is for William, this is Scott Simpson, certified personal trainer with Achieve Fitness USA calling on behalf of (equipment store name) to schedule your complimentary in-home training session. Please feel free to contact me at your earliest opportunity (your phone number, then repeat your number)." Always leave your number twice, say it the first time at normal speed, the second time a bit slower. The easier you make contacting you the more people will do it.

Performing the demo

Once you know the specific piece(s) of equipment the prospect has purchased be sure to become completely familiar with it. If you are not, get into the store and spend some time with it/them and have one of the sales staff give you a sales presentation on it. It improves your knowledge and endears you to the store.

Also have a quick list of exercises you feel comfortable demonstrating and a plan for introducing the prospect to the equipment. We typically have exercises for the chest, back, shoulders, biceps, triceps, legs, and abdominals prepared and ready to roll. Then if need be you can adapt "on the fly". If the demo is on a piece of cardio equipment be certain you know how to program the machine and demonstrate its electronic capabilities.

So now you're on the front door step. First introduce yourself, of course they know who you are (after all they were expecting you), but always greet prospects with a firm handshake and a business card. En route to the home gym area create some small talk, complimenting on the home is always a winner. Comment on any pets you see (or its evident they're there even if unseen), notice pictures on walls as they make easy small talk openings about family particularly children and/or grand children. Always find something positive—anything. Get off on a good foot.

The first twenty minutes should be predominantly conversational. Get a little more information on their goals. Ask open-ended, "why" type questions and focus on building a comfortable rapport.

The second twenty is devoted to the actual equipment demo. Remember, you are not going to leave them with an exercise prescription. Sometimes you will get prospects who want just that. When this happens you have to walk the tight rope of answering their question without giving them what they want. Something along the lines of, "In order to provide you with an exercise program I'd need far more information than I have.

Everyone's body and goals are different. I'd be happy to set up a time to come back and perform a thorough evaluation to get you started on a customized program though. Let's table that discussion for just a few minutes." This will usually suffice. Rule of thumb is to keep answers to specific questions general, if more information is requested use that as an opportunity to discuss the benefits of the profile session — which is a paid session, not complimentary.

As you are approaching the 45 minute mark, without being rude, act as though you have another appointment and begin preparing to leave. Ask them if they would like to set up a time to complete their profile session. Explain the information given today was general. To get more specific and to get the most from their investment, you recommend completing a profile session, which includes a program design specific to them. Always get a reason to call back, if they decline to schedule the profile session on the spot, then slipping them into your schedule in the next few weeks is that reason.

Here's an example of how to properly demonstrate and discuss a squat with a prospect. Discuss the benefits of performing the squat and how it is a motion very relevant to every day activities. Keep it brief, just a few sentences is plenty. "Squats are not only important for shaping and toning the muscles of the legs its an activity we perform everyday, you do everyday like sitting down in a chair, getting out of a car and yes, getting off the toilet. If the gym they've purchased as a squat setup or attachment, show them how to use it. If not then demonstrate a good wall or free standing squat.

Follow this pattern for other lifts and exercises. Demonstrate then discuss real world applications. Discussing core integration and why it matters is also a good strategy. In the event the prospect has an injury of some sort, use that as a selling point. Safe injury rehabilitation is an excellent motivating factor for hiring you. Remember, discuss it but don't give away the farm. You still want them to have a reason to hire you.

Taking excellent care of the prospect is always priority one, not landing a new client. Remember, even if they decline to hire you, you still have the relationship in place with the store and the store will sell more equipment which means you'll get more demos. However, one negative report back to the store from a prospect can kill the relationship with the partner and that's too valuable a thing to risk. Always be on time, always be polite and never, ever tell off-color jokes, improperly compliment a prospect, etc. Losing your partner could cost hundreds of thousands of dollars over the years to come, never risk it.

Even if the partner sends you on a demo that's well out of your traveling range, say 45 minutes or more away. It's well worth it for you to suck it up and go. Generating loyalty and good will with this power partner will always pay off. One call from a customer complaining about your no-show could be all it takes for you to be shown the door. Make the sacrifice, keep the partner's customers smiling and your rewards will come in due time.

Just like prospective vendors, never give up on a prospective client either. Often times demo sessions pay off immediately, often times they don't. If a prospect does not sign on for your in-home services, that's ok. They'll appreciate you graciously not pressuring them. Add them to your email newsletter campaign, Christmas card list and whatever on-going marketing efforts you have going. As your company grows and you hire new trainers, give them the past demos list as a leads list to begin prospecting. Have them simply call past demos, introduce themselves as a new trainer in the company and they were wondering how the fitness program was coming and would like to offer a half-priced profile session. These strategies work. Chances are good that one day they'll come on board or pass your contact information on to someone who's looking for training services. We have had demo sessions from four years ago call to schedule sessions because they're frustrated by a lack of progress and remember how excellent our in-home presentation was.

Working with multiple stores

The question often comes up, "Can I have this complimentary demo session relationship in places with more than one store at a time?" The answer is yes, and no. We recommend you develop a relationship with one store, preferably one with multiple locations. Your ability to work with what are essentially competitors depends in large part on the size of your market. In a city with millions of people like Houston or Miami or Los Angeles, it's quite conceivable that you could work with more than one store and they will never be the wiser. However in a small to medium-sized market this is not the case. Store owners know one another and talk frequently, as does management. Remember, your pitch to the store is that you are providing them a competitive advantage. If you're providing the same things to every store, then there really is no advantage. You risk the loss of good will if the stores for whom you're providing services find out about it and feel slighted. Instead of having one good solid relationship you could end up losing all of them. And once that bridge has been burned its nearly impossible to rebuild.

The key to making this vendor work is diligent effort in relationship building. If you do locate a store with more than one location, which is ideal, whatever store locations you plan to service need see your face on a regular basis. Chances are very good that if you're successful in one store the others will want to use your services also. Visiting the stores on a weekly or bi-weekly basis is crucial. This will create a level of trust and familiarity. Keep in mind, the store's sales reps can also be your sales reps. Once they're comfortable with you, you become a part of their pitch. "Tell you what Mr. and Mrs. Jones, if you can make a decision to purchase this gym today I'll arrange to have one of the very best personal trainers in the city come right to your house. We have a relationship with Dale Halbrook, who normally charges $80 an hour for in-home private training sessions. If you give me a credit card today, I'll arrange to have Dale come out on our dime." Boom. The sales rep has just built you up, pre-sold your services and warmed up the prospects for you.

This is why face time in the store(s) is necessary. For years fitness professionals have been going into equipment stores and asking if they can put business cards on the desk. It doesn't work. The store is going to refer the trainers they like and have relationship with. Your cards sitting on a counter is not relationship, its using. We even bring in lunch or bagels and cream cheese from time to time. Offer to help out on the floor cleaning machines or helping to tear down and set up as models change or get sold. These can be some of the most important minutes you'll ever invest.

Partnering with equipment stores in other ways

Offering demo sessions is a tremendous business building tactic, but there are other ways to fully exploit this relationship and glean even more business. Spend some time brainstorming on how your mobile fitness training company can really maximize these relationships. Remember retailers are always looking for a competitive edge and one way to get that edge is by working with a company like yours. Below are some ideas we have successfully employed in our home market, feel free to try these and come with others of your own as well.

In-store body fat testing

Setting up a body fat station in the store and providing complimentary BMI analysis is an excellent promotional tool. The store can, and often times will, ad the promotion to their local advertising. "FREE body fat analysis at this Saturday's President's Day Sale!" This is a nice value-add for the store, provides you with free marketing, and puts prospective customers and clients into both of your databases. And all you have to invest is a little time.

This system was developed by fitness guru Phil Kaplan and is very strong. We have successfully used it in our local business several times. This system can be used in equipment stores but not necessarily limited to such. Body fat table promotions have been set up in mall kiosks, at conferences, hotel lobbies, therapist offices, event centers, charity vents, retirement homes, colleges and high schools, restaurants and just about anyplace there is adequate foot traffic.

Always begin by asking yourself what the prospective client wants. Generally speaking what people want when they seek out a fitness professional is to feel better, change self-destructive behaviors, and to achieve a potential they know they have and are falling short of. Notice "to be associated with a number" is not on the list. People don't *want* to know they're 33% fat. They may think they want numbers, but they don't! They want feelings! They often want to trade bad feelings for good ones, such as low self-esteem for confidence, but they don't really want numbers. Feelings are fragile and numbers have the power to send those feelings in the wrong direction.

Without a point of comparison a body fat reading has no meaning. Why are we measuring fat? To establish a baseline, right? To determine where someone is right now so we have that reference point to compare future measurements to. Take and record caliper measurements but forget about the conversion formula. Just record the numbers. You now have a baseline. Twelve weeks later perform a re-test. Now convert both the early and current measurements into body ft percentages. If working with a client, well they better have dropped some. If working with prospects and there is little or no change, use that as a motivating factor for inspiring them to hire you.

The body fat table is simply a table, but one that knocks down the invisible shield. Put a sign on the table says, "DO YOU KNOW YOUR % BODYFAT?" Place it on the table along with anything interesting that might draw people over. Put a few bottles of supplements that you're comfortable explaining, or a few common foods that you can use to explain supportive nutrition or label reading. Put some papers that might stimulate interest.

Sugar and/or fat content examples

Another effective and easy to do in-store promotion is sugar and fat content examples. This is another promotion we have used with great success in our home market. Simply line up some commonly consumed, sugar laden products — like soda or yogurt — then measure out the exact amount of sugar contained in each and place that amount of refined white sugar into a clear container placed next to the item in question. It makes an excellent visual. The same can be done for fat content. As a substitute for actual fat you'll need to use a substance that does not liquefy at room temperature but has a similar look and consistency as fat. Hand cream works well as does mayonnaise.

Blood pressure or other testing

Any kind of health and fitness relates services or testing you can offer is beneficial. It helps the store bring people through the door to bring customers in the door, ads some action, some "sparkle" to the sales floor, plus gets you valuable face time with the store's ownership, management and staff. Blood pressure testing is also quick, easy and cheap. All you really need is a blood pressure cuff (and know how to use it). Remember, there are two goals — to promote your services while at the same time helping store gain foot traffic and ultimately gain sales.

In-store workshops

Workshops are one of the best ways to gain business and add value to the store. The store's ability to advertise, "EATING RIGHT ON A TIGHT BUDGET WORKSHOP FROM NOON TO 1:00 THIS SATURDAY" is a tremendous asset for them. There are all kinds of workshops you can come up with and get rolling with very little effort and often no investment. "Proper exercises for seniors", "20-minute in-home circuit for busy moms", "Are all carbs created equal?" and literally dozens more. Get creative, you'll be surprised how open-minded the store management will become as you come up with more ideas.

Sport-specific workshops

Sport-specific in-store workshops are another gold mine. Examples of a sport-specific workshop might be "Shape up for the ski season" or "Improve driving distance golf workshop". Most sports have movements that are peculiar to that sport. A tennis backhand or a golf swing are not everyday motions.

Advertising the ability to come to a workshop and learn how to stretch, strengthen muscles specific to the golf swing is a sure-fire hit with golfers. The same holds true for just about every recreational sport. The golf and ski workshops are two we've done locally. See the appendix for example flyers for each.

Say what you'll do, do what you say

When it comes to store relationships never exaggerate (because you need to deliver on promises), but make it clear that this relationship will benefit the store as well as your business. Let them know that your goal is to first grow their business because in so doing, your business growth becomes inevitable. Know which side of the bread your butter is on. When the store succeeds, you succeed.

Refer customers to your store(s) at every opportunity. It helps grow the relationship. If you have a friend or family member just looking for one ten pound dumbbell, be sure and send them into the store and instruct them to let the staff know they were referred by you. The store management *will* notice, just as they will notice if you never send customers in.

Past customers lists

Perhaps the ultimate coup for the mobile fitness services business owner is a relationship with an equipment retailer that is so strong the retailer is comfortable turning over it's past customers database. For stores that have been in business for years, possibly decades, this list can be very long indeed. Getting your hands on it along with the store's permission to begin marketing to it is almost a guaranteed way to acquire clients.

Needless to say this requires a lot of mutual trust. The store management must be certain you are going to handle the list professionally or turning the names of their clients over could come back to bite them, big time. Convince the store to grant you access to the past clients list by bringing a business plan to them and show them the intent. Everyone appreciates an organized, professional approach to business. Communicate the fact that your goal in working this list is, yes, to gain new clients, but also to bring these past customers back into the store. "I will inform them that we are now conducting free body fat testing and fitness analysis in the store every other Saturday. I'll explain to them that having a treadmill is a good start, but a complete fitness program must include resistance training and set an appointment to view current gym sets that are on clearance." You get the idea.

As an independent personal trainer and not a store sales rep, we have a level of credibility that store personnel do not. We can refer past clients in without coming off as "salesy". "Mr. Anderson, your gym is incomplete. If you really want to do this right then you need a stability ball and a set of dumbbells. Go back to the store and talk to Sherry, let her know you're working with me. Once you have everything you need, I'll come back and design a program that will meet all of your fitness needs."

Using this approach, if you send in a handful of past clients, some that perhaps have not been in the store since their purchase two years ago—trust us, that store will begin bending over backwards to get you past client leads. You are now working what is essentially and old dead-leads list and breathing life into it. You are doing their work for them. Any sales person is going to jump all over that.

Once you have the list, a polite, introductory phone call announcing the relationship between your company and the store and a complimentary session is sure to net at least a handful of consultation sessions. From there, landing clients is up to you.

Once you have the past customers list put a system in place whereby the store provides you a monthly list of everyone who has purchased equipment. Give them all the same courteous call and offer and soon the system will be in place. The store is now feeding you a regular diet of fresh client leads. You now have the ability to get in front of prospects without having spent any money on advertising what so ever. Is all this worth a few lunches and bagels a month? You bet!

Here's an example of a prospecting call to someone from a past clients list, "Hello, my name is Frank Johnson, I'm a certified personal trainer with Fit Bodies. Fit Bodies has partnered with Goodson Fitness, where you purchased a treadmill last year. On behalf of Goodson we are offering all past clients a complimentary in-home fitness session. There is no cost to you, I just have to put you on the calendar and one of us will be happy to come out."

This activity can and will increase your client base drastically. Never do any sales on the phone, the conversation is all about how Goodson is making this service available and you're just wanting to schedule them on Goodson's behalf. If you try to sell them on in-home personal training at this point things can get awkward. No one likes telemarketing calls. And all it takes is just one past client to call Goodson's, ask to speak to the manager and say, "Why have you guys sold my name to a telemarketing firm? I don't appreciate being called by your sales reps in my home!", and you're done. Asking if they've been using the treadmill (or what ever piece of equipment the purchased) is fine, but don't go much beyond that.

Exclusives

When presenting the business system, questions we commonly field revolve around exclusivity. "Should I be exclusive with the store?" and "Should I request the store be exclusive with me?" ("Should I request they use no other in-home personal trainer?")

Yes you should be exclusive with a given store or chain of stores if there's more than one under the same ownership, but not until you feel like the relationship has been adequately developed. Once things have begun rolling and both sides are realizing some significant traction, sit down with the store ownership or management and discuss the benefits of them going exclusive with you.

- All clients receive a guaranteed in-home session.
- They will receive 100% of referrals (new clients for the store).
- We have proven our ability to refer clients back into the store.
- They receive stability. The opportunity to use one company rather than multiple individual trainers is huge. Equipment stores have to track and trust different trainers, do they really want to do this?
- They have just one contact person rather than a list.

Concerning you going exclusive with them; if you feel the store has a lot to offer in the form of growth and referrals then going exclusive makes sense. There's not a lot of point in continuing to fish when you've already got one on the hook. Spreading your service across too many different stores (which can be as few as two) can come back to bite you and the loss of loyalty is a bitter taste that's not soon forgotten. Double-dealing with two stores can end up costing you the relationship with both.

Informing a store that you are willing to go exclusive with them and provide them with all of your marketing and training expertise can sound very appealing to them. Knowing that you will refer business to them exclusively has a lot of appeal, after all you are a health and fitness professional and they sell health and fitness products. It's a hand-in-glove fit.

Attached in the appendix is a sample agreement which we have used successfully in the past for providing equipment stores with an exclusive. Copy and use this or come up with your own, either way, exclusive agreements can workout very well.

Motivating the sales staff

To make this business model go, one of the most important things you must do is keep the sales staff at the store(s) motivated to continually refer demos to you. Sometimes sales persons just forget to offer you. If that happens you just missed a new client opportunity. Make sure to always be marketing yourself and keeping yourself and your services visible and in the front of the store sales staff's minds. Systemically performing each of the following will go a long way toward accomplishing this.

- Spend time at the stores. This is the best way to develop the relationship and keep staff motivated. Hang around. We'd even advise working out on the sales floor from time to time. Remember, the equipment on the sales floor is fully functional. Electronic machines are plugged in and weight machines are fully assembled. So make plans to put your personal workouts in *at the store*. It's a clever move. Not only do you accumulate face time with the staff, you familiarize yourself with the equipment lines the store sells plus you are available as a sales tool. Say a customer comes in and is looking around the sales floor while you're working out. Here you are, a fitness professional with your own in-home gym, memberships at two or three different gyms around town, but you choose to come here to train! That's what I think of the equipment they sell here at Fitness Gallery, I like it so much that I come here rather than go to the YMCA down the street. That's like going into a restaurant and seeing that Emeril eats there. Talk about credibility.

- Call the sales staff weekly, ask how are things going and if you can help with anything. Do they want to run a body fat table this weekend or any other promotions? Do they need any help today? Often times machines on the floor need to be moved around, placed into the front display window, etc. It's entirely possible that only one sales rep is on duty in the middle of the day on a Tuesday — and those things are heavy. Offer to come down and lend a hand. On the way in pick up a Starbucks.

- Have an on-site mail box. Somewhere in the back workings of the store have an inbox where staff can place notes or other items for your attention. This weaves you into the fabric of the in-store family and makes you look and feel more like an employee yourself.

- Don't over do it, but come to the store during known slow times. Stopping by to spend time getting to know the staff at 11:00am on a Saturday is a bad idea. They have customers who need attention. Mid-morning and mid-afternoon on weekdays are typically slow and staff can afford a few minutes. Stop in and say "hello" during these times. Especially in the winter (if you're in a cold weather state). They may actually appreciate the company.

- Develop a fax system for repetitive communications. Below is a letter we developed that gets faxed to the stores every Friday morning (Letter 3.0). This reminds them to refer us and contact us if they need anything.

Letter 3.0

Your Logo
Your address
Your telephone number
ABC Equipment Store Sales,

I hope you had a phenomenal sales week. Please remember to refer your Solid Body Fitness trainers to every client who purchases equipment. This is to benefit you and Solid Body. We will provide all of your customers a complimentary in-home session in which we will demonstrate the benefits of their new purchase. We also strive to refer your customers back to you for potential add-ons and up sells.

Remember to offer this session as a service ABC Equipment Store is providing because ABC Equipment Store wants them to accomplish their personal fitness goals. Solid Body Fitness will represent you with the utmost professionalism. We do not do sales during the complimentary session. It is strictly a session to orientate them on their equipment, provide them with expert advice and motivation.

We guarantee the quality of the session and trainer. We will take great care of your customers and get them back in the store to buy more equipment over time.

If you need any customer coupons contact us at 720-555-1212 and we will promptly deliver them to your store.

We are here to help grow your sales volume through repeat customer sales. Please do not hesitate to contact me should you have any questions or concerns.

Yours in Fitness,
Frank Rotella
Solid Body Fitness

Other profit centers

Having an excellent relationship in place with an equipment store that provides a steady diet of demos is a wonderful thing, however it's not the only thing. When partnering with an equipment store other opportunities abound. Expanding your relationship with the equipment store can quickly lead to other lucrative, mutually-beneficial arrangements. The good news in all of this is that many equipment stores already know that having relationships with personal trainers can be beneficial. Now all that's up to you is to convince them why working with you is their best option. The more business-building systems you can put on the table, the greater the chances they will work with you and possibly agree to become exclusive. Here are other services we have successfully offered equipment stores.

Exclusive marketing CD and/or DVD

Creating a CD or DVD with educational information on it is an awesome maneuver and not at all expensive to boot. The CD/DVD can market your services and be provided to the store sales staff for use as a complimentary handout. This allows the staff to provide extra value to the customer by handing out a free CD/DVD that has a motivational talk on it, by you, on a topic relevant to fitness and exercise. Co-brand the CD/DVD and/or its cover with yours and the store's logo. End the CD/DVD with contact information on how to set up a complimentary in-home consultation.

The CDs can be printed on your computer at home with labels for as little as a dollar each or can be professionally printed for even less if purchased in bulk quantities. Visit www.dupication.com for more information or just thumb through the local yellow pages.

If you don't own a digital recorder one can be purchased for under thirty dollars. Then set up a discussion outline and talk about something that will get the customer's attention and educate them. Or have a friend or family member sit in as an interviewer and record the CD/DVD in a question and answer format. Topics abound; "The five keys to permanent fat loss", "Why weight training matters." Create something educational for the customer and always end with information on how to hire you.

Once completed, give the sales reps a specific quantity amount and track the success of each sales rep's distribution efforts. This will show you which reps are really pushing your services. Little things like offering a free exercise CD/DVD can help them close deals. Smart sales professionals will jump all over it. Those who ignore this free tool are probably near the bottom of the production pile.

Open an in-store studio

Most all fitness professionals have the goal to one day open a private studio. And most all who do fail for one reason. Rent! It comes due whether clients are showing up (and paying) for workouts or not. One way to circumvent this problem and endear yourself even more to your equipment store(s) is to leverage the relationship and open an in-store studio.

The high cost of rent is a problem for many equipment stores too. An in-store studio arrangement can be a solution to both party's problem. Opening a studio inside the equipment store is a proposition that's got win-win written all over it.

The equipment store wins

The store realizes more foot traffic as our clients coming for training sessions must walk into their store. On the way through they may spot something and buy it. More traffic always equals more sales. Assuming that you have a sub-lease agreement, the store is mitigating a portion of their rent—even if your sub-lease is on a non-cash basis. (More about this in a moment.) The sales reps also know you are in the store on a more constant basis to provide customers expert advice, run promotional programs, maintain a bulletin board, etc. They also have more activity in the store which creates energy. High energy is an intangible but always a good thing. There's nothing worse than customers walking into a "dead zone" store. Last and possibly most importantly, the store gets a valuable sales tool. If a customer is waffling on a big-ticket purchase, the store can offer to have the piece of equipment set up in the studio. The prospective client can hire you for a handful of sessions and train on the piece of equipment before committing to purchase it. This keeps the client from walking out the door to "think about it" (sales death sentence), gets you a small session sale and access to a potential new client.

And often times the store has the necessary square footage for a studio already available and just not being utilized. So now you are showing ownership how to take revenue-draining square footage and convert it into revenue-producing square footage. That's a language all retail store owners speak.

You win

Since you're in the store you still are receiving the potential in-home referrals. Any equipment you place into the studio may be provided on a gratis basis or at the store cost, thus saving you thousands of dollars. Its quite likely you can make a rent arrangement that is based on a percentage business, meaning you're not coming up with cash out-of-pocket. And there's typically no credit check or security deposit requirement.

Having an in-store studio also gets you a free sales staff. The store sales staff will make mention of the fact the store offers on-site training and, as mentioned above, may even use the studio facility as a closing tool. That means they're selling *your* services even though they don't work for you. That's another way of saying "free".

Approach

Begin by just working on the relationship for growing your mobile personal training via the in-home demo system. Show the store management the quality of your services and business plans and commitment to the partnership. Once they begin to feel comfortable with the relationship, then go in and talk to the owner about taking the partnership to a higher level with an in-store studio. Set up this meeting and come into it with a written plan that is organized and detailed—especially the financials portion. Include a sales forecast and always remember, this has to make sense of the store owner. Highlighting the financial benefits for her is what will put this plan over the top. Talk win-win. Your ability to provide additional income, increased traffic, develop more exclusive trainers, and a reliable back-up revenue stream is what will prick their ears up.

Be certain the store has space to accomplish your goals. About 600 square feet is all that's necessary. In most situations 600 square feet can be used by two trainers, each working with one client, simultaneously. Double that, 1200 square feet, can comfortably be used by four or five trainers at a time. Having some office space is valuable as well. If you can, negotiate a small space big enough for a desk, computer and three chairs.

Insurance and liability

Many stores will say they can't do this because of insurance. Foresee this objection, be prepared and have that base covered. Stop them and say, "My insurance policy will cover all sessions and equipment in use. Here is a copy." Doing this in first meeting is very important as it casts a long, strong shadow of professionalism. They will want to see you are business-minded, and those are the sorts of individuals owners seek to be in partnership with. Go to www.trainerinsurance.com to receive a policy and certificate for the studio very quickly. The policy will specifically name the store as an "also insured" location, which puts the owner's mind at rest.

Chapter Six

Other Business Growth Tactics

While vendor relationships, especially those with equipment stores, are tremendous growth opportunities they certainly aren't the only one. Creating and using other resources to grow business should be taking place concurrently with the vendor development process. Several business development strategies covered in this chapter should be employed while pursuing quality vendors. Vendors are good and vendors are important, but its foolish to ever place all of one's eggs into a single basket, no matter how well constructed that basket appears to be.

Develop a promotional CD and/or DVD

We recommend everyone develop a CD/DVD about you, your company, what you have to offer and with detailed contact information. The format for this electronic media can be very simple. Complexity and a lot of techno-wizardry isn't nearly as important as content and effective delivery. Here are the sections your CD/DVD needs to contain.

- Welcome - introduce yourself and describe what you are going to talk about on this CD/DVD.
- Motivation – provide incentive to hear the CD/DVD out. Motivate the listener to complete the session.
- Feature/benefit analysis of your services – tell people they are fat lazy slobs who need some accountability in their lives if they're ever going to get into shape. Ok, well not in those exact words. Use this section for description of services provided; kettlebell classes, pilates, in-home,

weight reduction, etc., plus a discussion of why these things are important, like living longer (a benefit of exercise).

- Contact information – all contact information should be included, especially your website address, and a description of how they can hire you.

Add any other information you feel necessary. Remember, the goal of this CD is to educate prospects and get them excited about working out in the home.

In the previous chapter we covered information on actually making the CD/DVD. In either case have a basic script that you're following but not reading. For a CD you'll need a digital voice recorder. If you feel comfortable with your speaking voice then record it yourself, it adds credibility as you are both the trainer and the owner. If you don't feel comfortable or have a voice like Minnie Mouse use anyone you know who has an excellent voice tone.

If the quality is poor the recording can be professionally edited. Yes it will cost a few bucks but remember, you may be handing these CDs out for years and years to come. A one time investment in editing can still be paying off five years from now. A professional editor can remove pauses, take out background noise and static and perform a host of other functions that will greatly improve the quality of your presentation.

A quality digital video recorder will be necessary for DVDs. And if at all possible, have the DVD recorder mounted on a tripod or some other such stationary device rather than being hand held. The shakiness inherent in hand held recordings can be a real distraction and may even cause some people to turn it off all together. A steady camera provides a far more professional appearance.

Marketing on the world wide web

If you are a fitness professional in this day and age you must have a quality website. Period, end of story. Unless you are content with little to no growth, the days of being able skate by without one are gone. If your primary three competitors all have websites and you do not, guess who's at the bottom of the totem pole. If you don't have a website yet, get on it!

The website itself must contain a biography of the trainer as well as locations serviced. The prospective client will want to know as much about you as you do about them. Don't make them search. Make sure the web page explains all services offered. And gift certificates are often a good idea.

Once the website is launched have a web form on it for customers who come from vendors. This way when ever a customer purchases equipment or is referred in some way from a vendor they have the option of calling or filling out the web form to schedule their consultation or demonstration session. This is critical, some customers will not call but will visit a website in a heartbeat.

The web form needs to be concise yet still collect all vital information. Be certain to get name, phone number #1, phone number #2, address, email address, dates and times available for the complimentary session and maybe even an optional goals section so you gather some useful tidbits to discuss when you call.

Hiring trainers

Hiring people to work for and with you is one of the most important aspects of growth. Doing everything yourself is a mistake if for no other reason than it is income-limiting. No one can work all the time. If nothing else you've got to sleep sooner or later. And, try as we may, we've never been able to locate anybody willing to pay us for sleeping. But when you have a team of people working for you, the ability to earn while not working becomes very real. That's the difference between an independent trainer and a business owner. A business owner's business makes her money instead of her always having to be the one making her money.

We always recommend hiring independent contractors (versus employees), at least at first. It makes more sense and is far less of a hassle from an accounting and payroll perspective. Independent contractors are paid via an IRS form 1099 Misc., which is a much simpler filing than that required for W-2 employees. (For more information a detailed description of employees versus contractors, accounting and IRS guidelines is provided in chapter four of book #2 of The Success Express, "Launching Your Very Own Fitness Company"). You train them, show and teach them your system. Demo calls come in to you and you dole them out to the contractors. Until a trust relationship is built, always handle the actual customer calls yourself. When the trainer converts a demo into a new client, have them under a contract which states the company retains a percent of flat rate of billings and the rest goes to the trainer.

Finding quality, qualified personal trainers to hire can be challenging. A lot of it depends on the market you are in. In larger cities there are literally trainers everywhere. But just because they're abundant doesn't mean the talent pool is very deep. Here are some places we're looked for and found people to hire:

- Local gyms
- Friends
- Colleagues in the business

- Internet
  - Craig's list
  - Local Websites
  - On-line ads
- Newspaper Ads
- Word of mouth

When you're a new mobile fitness business owner you probably cannot afford to pay a trainer a salary. Doing so would go against the philosophy of minimizing your overhead/risk. This leads to the option of paying them a higher percentage for doing sessions and possibly providing the opportunity to move into a management position and be placed on a profit sharing plan.

You'll find many trainers are not just looking for a training position but are looking for opportunity. The majority of personal trainers are club trainers, which means they may be making as little as $15 per class or session and have no real outlet for exercising or developing their business acumen other than working the weekly "fit shift." Show the right person that you will pay them more than any club in town in exchange for hard work and dedication to growing the business with you. Sooner or later you'll run across a diamond in the rough. Someone who just needs a little pressure and polishing and they can really shine—and help your business do the same.

Offer them independent contractor work and begin teaching them the system. Explain that the demo session is not a paid session but give them multiple opportunities each week gain new clients. A smart trainer with a keen business mind will accept this tradeoff immediately. After all, its better than marking time on the workout floor at the gym for minimum wage.

Hiring Duds

Hey, it happens. We hate to rip the industry which we ourselves are a part of, but the fact is there are more bad trainers out there than good ones. Not just poor trainers but people with next-to-no ethics or morals or who just plain aren't too bright. We've had all of the above. There is no shortage of people who will come aboard solely with the intention of stealing business from you, learning and stealing business-building ideas or other selfish reasons. If you continue to succeed and to grow it's unavoidable. We've hired what we thought was the nicest person in the world and they turned around and stabbed us squarely in between the shoulder blades. Not that we're down on the human race, not by any means, but the need to keep your eyes open is real. We all hope to only bring aboard quality individuals, however its important to live by the mantra, "Trust, but verify".

Having a rock solid non-compete agreement in place for all new hires is a must. Have it available in the new-hire meeting and immediately set the standard. Any and all clients the trainer lands are part of your organization. They are the company's clients, not the trainer's. If the company and the trainer part ways one day fine, but the clients stay. All new hires must sign a non-compete agreement. You can find many standard non-compete/non-competition agreements on the internet. See the example non-compete in the appendix of this book to get an idea of the wording in a typical non-compete agreement. We provide some great examples of legal agreements in the appendix but recommend consulting an attorney.

Its also not a bad idea to have the client sign a form stating you are the agency for the trainer. The form has your information and logo on it. It may be a bit over the top but it covers you legally from both sides of the fence.

Attracting quality trainers

People are like magnets, they tend to attract more of their own kind. Once you find the first quality hire, he or she tend to lead to the second, who leads to the third, and so on. First of all, look for team players who understand there are more important things in play than today's paycheck. You are starting (or expanding) a business and will need quality managers and staff. As things grow there will be the opportunity for greater responsibility. If you present the opportunity properly, a smart individual will recognize and want the chance to be a part of something with massive potential. Offer a greater payout than anyone in town, but with an understanding that we're selling out to the business vision. In most cases trainers are $15 - $25 of a $70 session. Flip that around. Offer the trainer $50 and you take the $15, so long as they agree to work the business and help it grow. This means helping design signs, going out on demos, spending time on the vendor store(s), etc. — all activity that does not pay anything *while they're doing it*, but results in $50 per-session clients.

Offering profit sharing

When you do come across a trainer with drive, ambition and possibly the business skills you seek, offer a profit sharing plan in exchange for agreement to perform specific duties and reach specific (performance) milestones. This will tend to motivate the ambitious and de-motivate the slacker, and that's a good thing. The cream *always* rises to the top.

For example, once you've taught a new person the vendor system have a plan in place whereby they earn a percentage of all business that comes in from clients referred by that vendor — whether the trainer is personally working with the client or not. So trainer Jeff goes out and lands Tiffany's Hair and Nails as a vendor. Tiffany's agrees to a raffle box, newsletter insertion and a few other promotional plays. Having won this month's raffle box entitling her to two free sessions, prospect Rachel (who was looking for a personal trainer anyway) enjoyed her two sessions so much decides to become a regular client. Client Rachel begins working with trainer Kendra because she prefers a female trainer. For every session Rachel does with Kendra, Kendra gets paid her session fee and Jeff earns 4% because Tiffany's is his vendor. Now Jeff is earning passive income, he's getting paid even though Kendra is working with the client. What does this do to Jeff's motivation to get out and set up six more vendors? And you, as the business owner, are getting paid on all of it.

Realize that trainer Jeff is the exception not the rule. Most personal trainers are great at training and can get clients results, but not necessarily all that great at marketing or developing and executing a business plan. If you can show the good ones how to gain clients and earn a residual income tomorrow off of work they did today, you're well on your way to developing a loyal staff. Make sure to have a presentation in place when you interview prospective trainers/managers. Show the equipment store business plan and vendor development plans. Structure is always good. And remember, just like clients vendors fall under the non-compete agreement. If the trainer goes away, the vendor relationship belongs to the company. For this reason its very important to get out and meet personally with any and all vendors, even those your managers land. Associate the relationship to the company, not to trainer Jeff.

Using interns

Having a strong internship program can increase the likelihood of picking up great trainers. This is a good route as it allows for grooming a trainer into what you are looking for from the ground up. There typically are no bad habits to unlearn. Often times by the conclusion of the internship, the intern already has the beginning of a client base and they can simply be plugged directly into both the company and system. Depending on the educational institution they may already have been around for 400 - 500 hours of work and are well on the way to developing a strong understanding of your business and are plugged into a vendor.

Attract interns with a strong program. One of our in-house business coaches, Darrell Morris, has worked with numerous interns and put a solid intern program in place for our company. The fourth book of "*The Success Express*" series deals specifically with how to work with and utilize interns to successfully build and grow a training business. It's a step-by-step process of how to approach educational facilities, acquire, run and hire on interns for a mobile training business. Take all or part of it and begin making plans to employ it in your business.

Do I really need trainers?

In most all cases, yes, particularly if you successfully execute the equipment store vendor strategy. When (not if) you begin working with an equipment store its inevitable that sooner or later the store is going to sell a piece of equipment to a customer who lives 68 miles from you. Equally inevitable is that they used the complimentary in-home personal training session to close the sale. When this happens, the customer *wants* that session and, having made a commitment to the store, you are on the hook to go out and do it. This is not only a drag because of the 3 hours out of your day and $13 worth of gas to travel the 136 miles, but you're not going to get a new client. Little is more frustrating than to know going in that nothing is going to come of this demo. Bottom line is, even if the customer wants to work with you, you don't want them. Unless they're willing to pay $120 a session they're just too far away for the relationship to make sense.

This is why you need trainers working for you in the company. People to cover different geographic areas that you don't want to or simply can't. And the retailer may have stores in other areas that you can put under the management of these trainers and thus save yourself the commute time and costs associated with maintaining those relationships too. You still need to show your face from time-to-time, but the daily ins and outs of relationship building can be handled by someone else while you just manage.

Five step hiring process

When the business grows to the point you are hiring trainers and/or interns you'll quickly learn that some trainers will stay with you forever and others, well—not so much. View people who come aboard then move on to something else as stepping stones.

It takes time to understand that the stepping stone process is a necessary one. And failure to realize this fact can result in a lot of unnecessary stress. Realize that few are the people you'll bring on board who ultimately workout long term. Although that's a goal, it's highly unlikely and from strictly a numbers point of view, it takes time.

Be prepared. As you begin to grow gain multiple trainers you'll begin to develop an intuition about which trainers are likely to be keepers and which are likely to be stepping stones. Stepping stones are an important part of the process, they grow your abilities as a manager and ultimately play an important role in getting to where you want to go. They can provide both income and growth for the business. Following the five step process will help you avoid as many of them as possible, but avoiding them all is not possible.

Step 1 - Preparation

Being prepared for an interview is as important for the interviewer as for the interviewee. Have all of your materials pre-produced, organized and ready to roll. A favorable first impression is a two-way street. The interviewee could be one of the previously mentioned "stepping stones", or they could be an ultra-sharp hard worker who is going to make you tens of thousands of dollars over the next few years. You never know which ahead of time, so focus on making a positive impression on everyone. It would be terrible if this interview were one of the superstars and your lack of professionalism scared them out of the hiring process during the first meeting. Here's a list of necessary items for the initial interview:

- Compensation plan
- Company rules and regulations handbook
- Interviewee's resume and/or application
- Brief description page on the company and what it has to offer

Before interviewing you must create these materials and they tend to grow in length as time goes by. Starting with a two or three page description, general compensation plan, company rules and regulations booklet is perfectly acceptable. As the business grows and progresses so will your materials. And always have at least something in the compensation plan about profit sharing, even if only to mention that it may be available one day. People admire forward thinkers. The goal with these materials is to show the trainer you have a business forming and it would be a good time for them to jump aboard.

Step 2- The interview process
Initial phone interview

Be certain the materials mentioned above are prepared. The person you are interviewing is going to want to see structure and a system in place. Having step one complete allows you to make and leave the impression that they are about to step into a business-building system. Once this is done it's very important to schedule a phone interview prior to a face-to-face interview. Your time is valuable, and eliminating people likely to waste your time can and should be done before they get the opportunity. In the phone discussion ask the following questions:

- Briefly discuss their resume and specific questions about their duties at the current and last employers.

- Always ask if they can produce at least two professional references from each of their last two employers. Lousy employees tend to burn bridges. Anyone who waffles at a request for recent past-employer references is throwing up a huge yellow flag. Perhaps not red, but definitely yellow.

- Find out where they live and which aspects of the company they are interested in working in (mobile, corporate, residential, studio sales). If you are considering them for work in your mobile fitness business, knowing where they are will help determine if they are a good fit geographically.

- Discuss vision—first theirs, then yours. What they are interested in? What are your goals with our company? This question will also reveal whether they've invested some time into doing homework on your firm. By now they should at least have visited your website and have some basic information about your business. The goal here is to get them thinking. Listen carefully to how they answer these questions. Is it with confidence or do they have no idea of what they want?

- One of our favorite questions is, "What self-improvement books have you read in the past year?" Its been said that "leaders are readers". Success driven people tend to read and seek to engage in other self-improvement activities on a regular, habitual basis. Studies have shown that most adults in lower economic classes in this nation have not picked up and read a book since high school. If an interview peels off the name of two or three or four excellent books they're read in the past year, there's very good indicator you may have a diamond on the phone.

If your instincts tell you this individual could be an asset, schedule the live interview. If not, tell them you will review their application and resume and get back to them. Then the ball is in your court to call them to schedule or not. Another way to go is to instruct them to contact you within two weeks, then wait and see how long it takes for them to do so. Those who contact you within a week are probably worth an interview. Those who call back in three weeks are probably a waste of time. Many will never get back to you at all. Good.

Initial live interview
Whether they make it to the live interview or not, be sure and keep a resume file. File their resume away for future reference—

you never know. Great record keeping is one of the keys to success.

Give them homework to complete prior to the interview. Instruct the applicant to review your website(s) and bring questions. Offering them the opportunity to email you questions can be important. Lazy people won't typically take this step. Let them know they can feel free to email you questions.

To begin the interview we need to go into their goals and the vision that was discussed on the phone. Begin getting an understanding of what they are about. Have a list of questions typed out, go thru them and take notes on what they say beneath each question. While you are gathering this information be thinking about where and how they would fit into the position you are discussing. Will they get along with sales staff at the vendor store? Would they fit better in another position? Have the best interest of the interviewee in mind first, the best interest of your company in mind second.

Next present the position available and I ask the hard questions concerning how they would handle specific situations that may come up in this position. Place them into imaginary but real-life scenarios and place them on the spot. "How would you handle a situation in which a customer...?"

Next discuss the compensation plan. Go through trainer pay, profit sharing and growth opportunities. Try to get a read whether they are interested in growing with us over the long term or just picking up clients. Are they all about getting paid today, or do they understand sacrifice today in exchange for bigger pay tomorrow? Ask where they feel they fit in best with the company.

If you're still not sure you want to hire them, schedule a Q and A. Tell them to read all company information and then email some questions based on this interview. It's a good way to signal that the interview is over without being rude. It buys you some time to think and allows you to evaluate their writing and critical thinking skills when analyzing the questions they come up with.

If you're sure this will be a good fit, do the Q and A right then and there. Spend extra time with them and begin to discuss specifics of this position. In most cases you still want to at least sleep on it and see if either of us have anymore questions tomorrow. If all seems well tomorrow, go ahead and the position and move forward with the hire on process.

Step 3 – Hiring

If interview went great and you are going to hire them, start by developing their file and putting the new hire on a 90-day plan. Never neglect to start a file for each and every trainer you bring on board. Document, document, document. Trust us, it can really save your bacon sometime. Present them with copies of their compensation plan, non-compete form, 1099 agreement, employee booklet (no matter how small), completed application and all other documents mentioned in this book and in "Launching Your Very Own Fitness Company". Get original copies with ink signatures and the new hire's resume and place all into his or her file. Here is a checklist to follow to make sure all documentation is in and nothing gets forgotten.

New hire checklist
Check off each when it comes in and is placed into the file.

- Personal Information Page - completed with resume and application attached.

- Non-compete Agreement - signed copy.

- Statement of Independent Contractor – signed copy.

- 90-day training form - this form explains the parameters of the 90-day training and goals program (more below).

- Compensation Plan – signed copy.

- Manager Plan – signed copy (if being hired into a management position).

- Ethical Conduct Statement – signed copy (especially important for trainers who will be working with in-home clients and/or managing a key vendor relationship).

- Copy of current certification certificate(s).

- Copy of current CPR certification.

- Copy of current first aid certification (optional).

90-day plan

One of the most important things you'll do when hiring trainers is setting them up for success. Growth cannot be haphazard, neither can their approach to business development be. Have them on a plan that develops 30, 60 and 90 day goals. Each goal being outlined and obtainable. This way expectations are known and activity levels can be monitored and adjusted to reflect progress, both successes and failures. See the 90-day plan found in the appendix. Use this one or create your own, but make certain not to ignore this step.

Structure and organization is one of the most important aspects of a business. This is the reason the 90-day plan is so important. If you are going to attract quality individuals you have to be able to show a system that paves the say to success. Being organized and providing structure for trainers will grow your income and business growth can be unlimited.

Now the first 90-days begins. During this time mentor the trainer to become successful under you and to benefit the company. Lay out the expectations and hold them to their agreements. Set short and long term goals for anyone who joins your team. We do it in a three-step process. Have trainers write down their 30, 60 and 90 day goals and use them to develop 30, 60 and 90-day activity requirements.

Step 4 - New trainer orientation

Every trainer needs to start with an organized approach meaning each trainer needs to go through an orientation process. What is an orientation system? An orientation system is a very important part to your business and hiring process. It affords an organized approach to starting a new employee or independent contractor on your team.

The new trainer orientation system is where you spend a specified amount of time training the new trainer on what they will be doing. This is where you go through important company information with them such as non-compete issues, company rules and regulations and reaffirm they have a complete understanding. You will also begin to provide the training they need to implement the system you have created with them in the 90-day plan.

New Trainer Orientation Packet

It is very important to have a packet with protocols you follow for doing an orientation with a new trainer. The appendix of this book also provides an example of what an orientation packet should look like.

Here's an example of an organized orientation letter and process:

Letter 5.0

Dear Applicant,

Congratulations on being accepted onto the Achieve Fitness USA team. To begin with Achieve Fitness USA every new trainer must go through an orientation process before they may begin working with our clients and business partners. This orientation is designed to will help you become an expert on the following topics:

Company Compensation Plan - You will receive an electronic copy of the company compensation plan and we will review your pay structure.

Company Rules and Regulations Packet - You will receive an electronic copy of the company rules and regulations packet which we will review together.

Performance Requirements – We will discuss the performance requirements and expectations as described in your 90-day plan. You will receive a copy emailed to you of our 90 Days to Success book.

Company Assets and Additional Revenue Streams - Achieve Fitness USA will review your company goals and orientate you on the various business revenue streams that are available.

Forms - Learn how to fill-out your pay form, auto credit card and billing forms, client agreements and more.

Mobile Fitness Training Demo and Consultation Training - Achieve Fitness USA has relationships in place with several fitness equipment retailers who provide us a steady flow of in-home client prospects. We will train you on performing demonstration sessions so you can begin obtaining clients for mobile training.

Studio Orientation System - We will spend 60 minutes orienting you on our studio operations.

Corporate and Residential Fitness Training - We will spend 60 minutes orienting you on how to pick up clients in corporate and residential centers.

A training approach like this provides a system for getting trainers started and learning about your business.

Step 5 - Trainer Development

Now that you have brought aboard the trainer, taken him/her through your training and orientation programs (steps 1-4) and begun to implement the 90-day program, it's time to start implementing the plan and work toward the goals in the trainer development section.

You must have an accountability program that includes both rewards and penalties to the trainers if they don't follow through on plans. Make them accountable. Where accountability lacks so do results. Make it very clear that it's the trainer's job to develop a client base with your help and assistance. Your job isn't to get clients for them. Your job is to provide the tools, training and relationships necessary. If you hold up your end of the bargain they won't have any problems acquiring clients. It's a fact in the personal training industry trainers who can network properly and implement a solid client acquisition system can become highly successful. Your job to make them accountable for actions and results as well as provide framework to become successful. If they're aren't lazy or lacking in social skills, they will.

In most cases it takes a trainer ninety days to one year to develop a client base. We've seen very "average" trainers come aboard and do it in six weeks simply because they have such strong networking and communication skills. We've also seen the opposite, great trainers who were unable to develop a client base just the opposite reason. No business and poor intrapersonal and/or networking abilities. Your job is to help them through the tough times, provide direction and opportunity and an environment in which they can flourish.

Provide new trainers the support necessary to become successful—within reason. Your job is to help make your people successful, after all the more successful they are the more you are, but know when enough is enough. If John starts as a independent contractor with you and John requires four hours of your time a day and it's been a year and he's only picked up a handful of clients, it's fairly obvious he's not worth the time you're having to invest into him. And its true, time is money. As the business owner you set the parameters so trainers know what to expect. Do this during the orientation period so things are clearly understood from day one.

Chapter Seven

No Equipment Necessary

Since the focal point of this book is emphasizing the wisdom and relative ease of opening a mobile fitness services company, it's very important that the reader be able to perform a complete session and design a complete fitness program utilizing sparse or possibly no equipment. Thus it only seems prudent that we provide some examples and resources for training clients in-home. Working in the client home sometimes requires knowing how to train clients without much or any equipment. Learn how to become excellent at no-equipment programming, and you're well on your way!

What follows are some very basic examples of exercises most clients can perform, regardless of conditioning level. And all of these can be done with next-to-no equipment and provide an excellent basis for beginning an in-home program.

Pushup

Begin in pushup position, on knees or toes. Perform 4 pushups, abs in and back straight. On the 5th pushup, lower halfway down and hold for 4 counts. Push back up and repeat the series — 4 regular pushups and 1 halfway — 5 or more times.

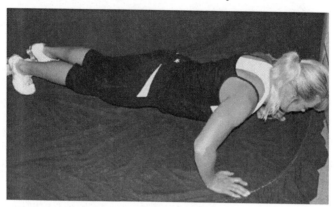

Medicine ball pushup

Place one hand on ball, lean toward the elevated side and perform the pushup. Beginners should always start on their knees. Alternate hands and repeat.

Staggered Pushups

For those not at an advanced enough level for a medicine ball yet, try a different version of the usual pushup by placing one hand on a phone book (or any other object) and the other on the floor. On knees or toes (and with body straight) lower down into a pushup and push back up.

Medicine ball tricep push up

Place both hands on medicine ball and attempt pushup. While dropping into the push up, focus on rubbing the elbows against the waist line. In the example photograph notice the feet are elevated for an added degree of difficulty. To simplify this movement keep toes on the ground or work from the knees.

Single-Leg Balance / Squat / Reach

Stand on one leg and hold as long as possible. If this is too easy, add a slight squat motion. Still too easy? Place an object on the floor, several feet in front of the client (a book, perhaps). Have them slowly squat down and reach out with one arm and touch the object and slowly return to an upright position. Stay on one leg at all times. Repeat on the other leg after a minute or so.

Adductor squat

Wide squat hold weight pointing directly down, squat down trying to touch weight (in this case a medicine ball but a dumbbell, kettlebell, gallon container of water, etc. can be substituted) to floor. As the squat is performed alternate lifting one heel up as the squat elevates press the heel down.

Backward Stride

Stand with feet together. Stride backward with one leg, while raising the arms to shoulder level. Lower the arms to the side and repeat with the other leg. Pick up the pace for more cardio.

Chair dips

You'll need two chairs, (or a bed and a chair or a counter, etc...) for this great tricep exercise. Place two chairs facing each other, about 3 feet apart. Sit on one chair with the palm of the hands down and gripping the edge of the chair. Place the heels on the edge of the other chair and support body weight using the triceps. Slide forward just far enough that the buttocks clears the edge of the chair and lower until the elbows are at 90 degrees. Do as many repetitions as possible.

For an added degree of difficulty try elevating the feet by placing them on a second chair.

Wall Sit

With back against a wall, and feet about two feet away from the wall, slide down until the knees are at a 90 degree angle. Hold the position as long as possible. This is great for ski conditioning.

Jump Lunges

Start in the lunge position – one foot forward and one foot back. Bend the knees, jump up high and switch leg positions. Use explosive, but controlled movements.

Reverse Crunch

Sit on the floor with knees bent. Hold hands out to your sides. Bring the knees toward your chest. Hold one second and repeat.

Jumping Jacks

The basic jumping jack is a good cardio and strength training exercise. Client can hold light dumbbells for added resistance and intensity.

Side Jumps

Stand with feet together. Jump to the right several feet, keeping knees bent and landing in a squat position. Jump back to the left and continue jumping from side to side. Use a small object to jump over if you like (book, pillow etc.).

Mountain Climbers

Begin on the hands and knees and get into in a sprinter's start position. Keep hands on the ground and push off with the feet, alternating floor placement (running in place) as long as possible. Be sure to keep the back straight, not arched.

Plank

Get into pushup position on hands and toes, or on elbows and toes. Contract the abdominal muscles. Keep the back straight (don't collapse in the middle) and hold this position for as long as possible.

Wall Squat-Thrusts

Lean into a wall with hands and keep the feet shoulder width apart several feet from the wall. Slowly lift one knee up toward the chest and back and then the other leg. As fitness level improves, increase leg lift speed and move weight onto the ball of the rear foot.

Abdominal Crunches

Lie on the back with knees bent and feet flat on the floor. Place fingertips to the side of the head just behind your ears. (Do not have the client interlock the fingers and therefore be "pulling" on the base of the neck). Push the lower back into the floor flattening the arch and hold. Curl up slowly so both shoulders lift off the floor a few inches, until shoulder blades slightly lift.

Hold for a count of two and return to the start position. Don't tuck the chin to the chest. Keep the head up.

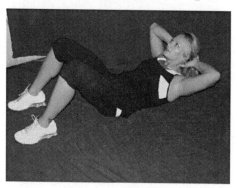

Oblique Abs

Sit with legs bent, back straight, arms extended straight out in front. Contract the abs and sweep right arm down and behind in a half-circle motion, leaning the torso back a few inches. Sit back up and repeat on other side.

Supermans

Lie on the stomach with arms and legs stretched out. Raise the hands and feet off the ground a few inches, hold a few seconds, and then lower. Repeat.

Walking Lunge

Start at one end of the room and take a long stride forward with the right leg. Bend down so the forward knee is directly over the toes and at a 90 degree angle. Raise up and repeat with the other leg across the room.

Shadow Boxing

Assume the position and go for a little shadow boxing. It's really a pretty decent way to get cardio and strength workout all at once. Focus on controlled movements (not flailing punches), stay light on the balls of the feet and keep the knees bent. Practice jabs, crosses, hooks and upper cuts. Hold a couple bottles of water or light dumbbells for additional more resistance.

Good Mornings

Stand with feet about hip-width apart holding phone book (or medium weight) straight up overhead. Keeping abs braced and knees slightly bent, tip from the hips and lower the torso until it is parallel to the floor, keeping the arms in line with ears. Lift up and repeat. Keep the abs braced throughout the move. If the client has any back problems, skip this move!

Pike Shoulder Pushup

This is a very advanced exercise, so use caution! Place toes on a step or stool and hands on the floor. Lift the body up into a pike position with hands directly under shoulders and the top of the head facing the floor. Bend the elbows and lower body into a pushup. Push back up and repeat. The move is shown on a ball which is even more advanced. Be careful!

Rear Delt Fly

With feet hip-width apart, tip from the hips until back is flat and parallel to the floor, abs braced. Lift the arms straight out to the sides to shoulder level with thumbs pointing up to the ceiling. Lower and repeat. Add light weights for intensity...if this hurts your shoulders, skip it!

Triceps One-Armed Pushup

Lie down on left side, hips and knees stacked. Wrap the left arm around torso so that left hand is resting on the right waist. Place the right hand on the floor in front, palm parallel to the body. Squeeze the triceps and push the body up. Lower and repeat before switching sides.

Squats on Tiptoes

With feet wider than hips, squat down and place hands on phone book in front. Raise up on the tips of your toes. Staying on tiptoes and fingertips, lift hips up towards the ceiling and straighten the knees as much as possible. Squat back down and repeat, staying in tiptoes the entire time. Modify by placing hands higher (on a chair or bed).

Lunge with Arms Overhead

Stand in split stance with feet about 3 feet apart. Hold phone book or weight straight up overhead. Bend the knees and lower into a lunge, bringing both knees to 90 degree angles, front knee behind toe. Keeping weight overhead, push back up and repeat before switching legs.

Single Leg Lift and Squat

Place hands behind the back and tip forward until back is parallel to the floor and flat, abs braced. Take right leg out to the side, resting on toe. Squat down with the left leg while simultaneously lifting the right leg a few inches off the ground and out to the side, leg straight. Straighten and repeat for all reps before switching sides.

Calf Raise

Stand on phone book with heels hanging off the back. Keeping body straight, lift the body up onto tiptoes by contracting the calves. Lower and repeat. This movement can be performed on the floor as well.

Exercise Programming with Resistance Bands

The resistance band is a very versatile and highly portable piece of exercise equipment and is a mobile trainer's best friend. In our careers as mobile fitness professionals we have consistently found the resistance band to be an indispensable asset when it comes to training clients in a mobile environment. The following section consists of some exercise and programming tips for working with clients using resistance bands.

Resistance Band Exercise 1: Chest

Place the band under a step or ball, lie face up holding handles in each hand. The elbows are bent and leveled with the shoulders, knuckles facing the ceiling. Contract the chest to push the arms up. (aka: flyes)

Repeat for twelve repetitions or appropriate work load for the client.

Resistance Band Exercise 2: Shoulders

Begin either standing or sitting, holding the band in its middle, arms straight out, hands a few inches apart. Squeeze the shoulder blades together, pull the band so that the arms are out to the sides. Return to the starting position and repeat, keeping tension on the band through out the duration of exercise.

Resistance Band Exercise 3: Arm - Triceps

Hold the band in both hands at shoulder level with the right arm bent so it's in front of the chest. Straighten the left arm. Keeping the left arm straight (to maintain tension on the band), contract the triceps to straighten the right arm. Return to the starting position and repeat. Switch sides and repeat.

Resistance Band Exercise 4: Arm - Bicep

Stand on the band, hold the handles with palms facing out. Keeping the abs in and knees slightly bent, bend the arms and bring palms toward shoulders in a bicep curl. (Note: position feet wider apart for more tension) Return to the starting position and repeat.

Resistance Band Exercise 5: Butt

Stand on the band feet shoulder-width apart. Keep tension on the band by doing a half-bicep curl. Lower into a squat, keeping the knees behind toes while pulling on the band to add tension.

Return to the starting position and repeat.

Resistance Band Exercise 6: Thigh

Tie a resistance band around the ankles so there're a few inches of band when standing with feet at hip-width apart. Take eight steps to the right, contracting the gluteals and outer thigh. Repeat on the other side.

Resistance Band Exercise 7: Back

Place the band around the back at its widest point and get a firm grip on the ends. Hold hands in front of the shoulders, slowly extend the arms, pulling on the band. Bring the hands together in front of the body, slowly release back to the starting position.

Resistance Band Exercise 8: Leg

Sit on a chair and tie the ends of the band in a square knot to create a circle. Slip the tied band over an ankle. Hold one foot steady while pulling the other foot out slowly. The foot can go to the side or forward. Release. Perform 8 to 10 reps on each leg.

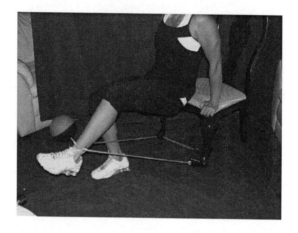

Resistance Band Exercise 9: Stomach

Tie a knot in middle of band and shut the knot in a door about two feet above floor. Lie on your back, knees bent and facing away from the door. Raise the arms overhead, grasp ends of band with both hands. Raise the head off the floor while pushing the left hand towards the right knee. Return to the starting position. Then raise the head off the floor and alternate (push the right hand towards the left knee). Hold each repition for three seconds.

No Equipment Needed
Program Examples

1. Climbing the Mountain

Warm up with 20-30Jumping Jacks, 20 Mountain Climbers (per leg) and 20 Squat, Thrust, Jumps. OR...5-10 minutes light aerobic activity like jogging, jumping rope, etc. Yes, this will seem like more of a workout than a warm up but we want the warm up to count.

The Workout:
You will be performing FOUR different movements. One lower body movement, one upper body pushing movement, one upper body pulling movement and one abdominal movement. In between each movement you will be performing either Jumping Jacks or Mountain Climbers for 10 repetitions.

The Routine:
Perform the routine in circuit fashion, taking little to no rest in between movements. Perform each movement for tenreps for the first circuit. Then go back through it but perform eight reps per movement except still perform ten reps for the Jumping Jacks or Mountain Climbers.

Next go back through the circuit again but this time perform six reps per movement while performing ten for the Jumping Jacks and Mt. Climbers. See the pattern?

Work your way down to two reps per movement and then work back up again (2,4,6,8,10). Once the client(s) is very well conditioned count down and then back up again by one's.

Lower body movement:
Choose one (body weight squats, walking or alternating lunges, jump squats).

Upper body pushing movement:
Choose one (pushups, bench or chair dips, plyometric pushups)

Upper body pulling movement:
Choose one (inverted rows, chins or pull-ups). This exercise will require either a pull-up bar of some sort, a table you can lie underneath and pull yourself up to or two chairs spaced apart with a strong rod in between.

Abdominal movement:
Choose one (crunches, reverse crunches/ leg raises, pushup position knee-ins, V-Up crunches).

An example of how it will look:

1. Squats x 10 (then 8, 6, 4, 2, 2, 4, 6, 8, 10)
2. Jumping Jacks x 10 (same reps each circuit)
3. Push Ups x 10 (then 8, 6, 4,2, 2, 4, 6, 8, 10)
4. Mt. Climbers x 10 per leg (same reps each circuit)
5. Inverted Rows x 10 (then 8, 6, 4, 2, 2, 4, 6, 8, 10)
6. Jumping Jacks x 10 (same reps each circuit)
7. Reverse Crunches x 10 (then 8, 6, 4, 2, 2, 4, 6, 8, 10)

2. Hellacious Hundreds
Warm up with 20-30 Jumping Jacks, 20 Mt. Climbers and 20 Squat, Thrust, Jumps or...5-10 minutes light aerobic activity like jogging or jumping rope.

Choose the same 4 exercises from the groups listed above. You'lll be striving to get 100 reps per each exercise. Start by performing as many body weight squats as possible until you can't get any more with correct form. If form begins to falter, STOP! This goes for every exercise!

In order to reach 100 reps you should rest for the amount of seconds it will take to achieve the corresponding rep count until you hit 100. For example if you have 50 reps left until you reach 100; rest for 50 seconds and then keep going until you can't get anymore. Use the same rest principle again then keep going until 100 is reached.

After finishing the first exercise, rest for 30-60 seconds and perform the next exercise in the same fashion and so on until all four exercises have been completed.

3. Crazy 8's

Mixing and matching exercises can be fun and motivating to the client while giving them more recover time.

Example:
7 squats, 1 push up
6 squats, 2 push ups
5 squats, 3 push ups
4 squats, 4 push ups
3 squats, 5 push ups
2 squats, 6 push ups
1 squat, 7 push ups

A Closing Note from the Authors

We would like to both thank and congratulate you for investing the money necessary to purchase this book and the time necessary to read it. That you have taken those two critical steps speaks volumes about your attitude and personal commitment to success.

Of course, the key now is taking the next step, namely, getting started implementing the system and doing the hard work. There is little profit in store for those who simply read this book and then pass judgment on the validity of its contents. Those who act, who take the principles and advice offered in these pages, and put them into practice — not sooner or later, not when the time is right, but do so now — are the ones who will find success in the fitness industry coming at them faster than most others dreamt was even possible.

Should you fall into the category of one who would take this process and act on it immediately, we have one more suggestion. If the content of this book makes sense, if you can see the vision we have put forth for success as a reality in your life, then you may be an individual with whom we'd like to work. As mentioned earlier, our company, Achieve Fitness USA, is experiencing amazing growth. In the past three years alone, we have expanded throughout Colorado into Arizona, California, Idaho, Illinois, Massachusetts, Nevada, New Jersey, New York, Texas, Georgia, Maryland, Washington, into Canada with multiple new locations likely to open while this book is in the process of being published.

Our primary method of growth is through licensing agreements with certified fitness professionals. We continuously seek out entrepreneurially minded, highly motivated individuals who are ready to take their professional lives to the next level. We review applications and conduct interviews on an on-going basis in every state of the U.S. and in Canada.

The purpose of this book is not to advertise our organization. Thankfully, through our own partnering and marketing abilities that's already been accomplished.

However, if you would like to make the leap into business ownership, we believe our program is the best of its kind. Building a company isn't easy, but we'd like to think we have much of the process figured out.

Our licensing partners not only learn how to take that step, but they learn many other vital and necessary skills in their quest for a six-figure (or more) income in the fitness industry. Skills such as how to develop multiple streams of income; how to maximize product sales; how to penetrate and launch boot camps, kids' camps, or corporate fitness services; and how to begin producing and selling fitness educational products that result in residual income for years or even decades to come.

There is a step-by-step process to go from being a solo trainer to running a diversified company with multiple divisions and revenue-producing arms. The Achieve Fitness USA Licensing Program now provides over 14 divisions that can be added to a new licensee's business structure, beginning on day number one. These divisions have great income potential and must all be managed properly. Like anything else in life, their performance only reflects the amount of effort that goes into developing them.

If you would like to explore the possibility of becoming an Achieve Fitness USA Licensing Owner, contact us today!

Visit www.AchieveFitnessUSA.com and fill in the requested information, or call 719-266-8040 or 303-721-0689. We will express mail an informational package and application to your front door.

We receive and screen dozens of applications each month. If you mention that you purchased and read this book, we promise your application will jump to the front of the pack. We support those who support us.

We believe there are cubic tons of unlocked potential in every human being. And further, that many who read this book are just one or two steps away from hitting the big time. Many people just need a small break, a nudge or a push, or to be surrounded by positive, success-minded people to move to the next level.

We're always looking for sharp, energetic additions to our team. Hopefully, you're doing the same. If so, we'd love to hear from you today.

About the Authors

Robert Raymond
- Fitness Business Coach
- Founder and President of RR Personal Training, Inc.
- Founder and President of Achieve Fitness USA
- Founder and President of Fundamental Fitness Products
- Founder of the Achieve Fitness USA Licensing Program
- Creator of the Biofitness Weight Management Program
- Creator of the Walkfitness Exercise Program as seen on TV
- Creator of the Personal Trainer in a Box evaluation kit
- Developer of the Power Training Program for Fitness Professionals
- Author of fitness and nutrition journals and guideline books
- Author of Mobile Personal Trainer Business Plan
- Established fitness presenter
- Bachelor of Science, Exercise and Sports Performance; Holistic Health and Nutrition
- Certified Personal Trainer, National Strength and Conditioning Association
- Certified Personal Trainer, American Council on Exercise

Bob has spent the past 15 years developing RR Personal Training, Achieve Fitness USA, and Fundamental Fitness Products. Each company has gained national recognition for its success and impact on the fitness industry in the United States.

In 2005, Bob changed gears and decided to spend his time mentoring and coaching other fitness professionals to become more successful as fitness trainers and businesspeople by launching the Achieve Fitness USA licensing program nationwide. For more on the Achieve Fitness USA licensing program, read "A Closing Note from the Authors" or visit www.achievepartnerprograms.com.

Derrick Wilburn

- Founder and President of Wholly Fit, Personal & Corporate Fitness Services
- Founder of Wholly Fit Ministries
- Fitness Business Coach
- Author of "The Battle Over Your Body" audio and DVD teaching series
- Author of "Gold Mine in Your Back Yard" CD teaching series
- Vice President of Program Management, Achieve Fitness USA
- Director of Channel Marketing, Fundamental Fitness Products
- Established motivational speaker and fitness presenter
- Master of Business Administration, Marketing
- Bachelor of Science, Marketing and Economics
- Certified Personal Trainer, 24/5 Complete Personal Training
- Twist Sports Conditioning Master Trainer

Derrick holds a Bachelor's of Science degree in marketing and economics, as well as a Master's of Business Administration from the University of San Francisco. A twelve-year veteran of high tech sales, marketing and business development, Derrick was very much at the forefront of the "tech boom" of the 1990s, living and working in the heart of California's "Silicon Valley" from 1989 until 2000. He became one of the youngest District Managers in the nation for a major player in the wireless data communication industry before moving on to become a Director at one of the world's largest ISPs (internet service provider), where he was responsible for building international distribution and co-marketing partner alliances. He has also served as a faculty adjunct in the school of business at the University of Phoenix, being university certified for teaching Marketing Principles, Marketing Strategy, Marketing Principles as well as Sales Force Management.

In January of 2001, he left high-tech and corporate America, relocated his family to Colorado, and founded Wholly Fit, a company and ministry dedicated to promoting physical well being. In 2002, he became a member of the Achieve Fitness USA team. Derrick is a lifelong proponent of healthy, active living, and draws upon his experience in the corporate arena to encourage teams and individuals to achieve lofty goals in the area of physical conditioning. He uses his formal educational background to aid, coach, and assist fitness professionals in the quest to move beyond being personal trainers to being business owners.

As an accomplished motivational speaker, Derrick integrates components of improved physical function into presentations for improving and perfecting organizations of all sizes. He is available for speaking engagements, seminars, or similar functions anywhere in the United States and Canada. For booking information, visit www.whollyfit.com or call 719-266-8040.

Julie Barger

- Founder of Bodz By Julz, Mobile Personal Training
- 17 years in Fitness Management
- 15 years in Train the Trainer
- Twist Sports Conditioning Master Trainer
- Associate Degree, Medical Assistant
- Bachelors of Sciences, Sports Medicine
- National Fitness Manager for Achieve Fitness USA
- Certified Personal Trainer, International Sports Science Association
- Corporate Fitness Director, Achieve Fitness USA

Out of high school, Julie immediately went to college for a medical degree. After giving birth to her first child, Julie found herself sixty pounds over weight and no closer to her medical degree. Having been athletic her entire life, she found herself applying at health clubs. She immediately became one of the top sales people in a large health club. The passion was born. She received an Associates degree in medicine, Bachelors in sports sciences and her ISSA certification. She became a "train the trainer" in sales and personal training. Having made several people quite wealthy while building their health and fitness clubs from the ground up, she finally realized she deserved the wealth she was creating. She broke out into mobile fitness training, created Bodz By Julz and has become one of the top mobile personal trainers in the Denver Metro area. She reaps the reward of not settling for second best, has created numerous success stories and is now National Fitness Director for Achieve Fitness USA.

Appendix

20xx Golf Fitness Seminars

Presented by Your Company Name, Personal
& Corporate Fitness Services

***Appletree Golf Club is pleased to
announce dates for our first ever,
"SHAPE UP FOR THE SEASON"
Golf Fitness Seminars***

- Improve power and overall golf game
- Proper stretching movements for key muscles in the golf swing
- Golf-specific core stability training and conditioning
- Most effective and efficient resistance training exercises for golfers
- Integration of off-balance training methods and equipment
- Critical chiropractic areas for golf injuries
- Personal attention in a small group setting (max. of 15 per seminar)

*Learn proper form and technique from Certified Fitness Professoinals through
hands-on training and the ability to interact directly with instructor(s).*

Attendees may sign-on for continuing personal instruction and also
purchase core conditioning and balance training equipment used in
the seminar at discounted prices!

Seminars begin at 10:00am on:
* May 27 * June 10 * June 17

Improve the most important piece of equipment you have! Cost
is just $99 per individual and includes seminar, training log and
exercise booklet.

Space is limited, see Earl McMullen or call
555-123-4567 to reserve a spot NOW.

Your Logo
Personal & Corporate Fitness Services
www.yourwebsite.com

SKI SEASON SHAPE UP BOOTCAMPS

Presented by Achieve Fitness USA, Personal/Corporate Fitness Services

- Improve power, balance, coordination and endurance
- Proper stretching movements for key muscles involved in skiing
- Ski-specific core stability training and conditioning
- Most effective & efficient resistance exercises for skiers
- Integration of off-balance training methods and equipment
- Critical chiropractic areas for ski injuries and injury prevention
- Personal attention in a small group setting (max. = 12 per camp)
- Child and adult appropriate

Learn proper form and technique from Certified Fitness Professionals through hands-on training with the ability to interact directly with instructor(s).

Camps include 2 workouts per week for 4 weeks plus at-home instruction. Attendees may sign-on for continuing personal services at discounted prices, and may purchase core conditioning and balance training equipment used in the camps at discounted prices!

Shape Up Camps begin next week!!

Improve the most important piece of equipment you have! Cost is just $289 per individual per camp. Camps are held at 2 locations.

Space is limited, call 555-1234 to reserve a spot NOW

Vendor Letter

Healthstyles Sales,

Please remember to refer your Achieve Fitness USA trainers to every client who buys any piece of fitness equipment. This is to benefit you and Achieve Fitness USA. We have a refer-back to the store program that will get the customer back in to see you and the client a FREE session to show them our skills and what we have to offer as professional fitness trainers.

Remember to offer this program as a service Healthstyles is providing for them because Healthstyles wants them to accomplish their goals. Achieve Fitness USA does not do sales in our demo session for Healthstyles customers. It is strictly a session to orientate them on their equipment, provide them with expert advice and motivation.

Please remember to exclusively refer us as your training team. We guarantee the quality of the session and trainer. We will take great care of your customers and get them back in the store to buy more equipment over time.

If you need any customer coupons contact us at 303-721-0689 and we will promptly deliver them to your store.

We are here to help grow your sales volume and get our company name in front of all customers. In order to do that we need to the opportunity to get in front of all customers.

Thank you,

Julie Barger
Achieve Fitness USA
303 721-0689

Partnership and Vendor Agreement

On the _____ Day of _____. Achieve Fitness USA and _____ agree to exclusively refer each other based upon both parties working with each other to provide a valuable referral network.

It is understood that it is of the responsibility of both parties to honor this exclusive partnership agreement.

Achieve Fitness USA offers personal training and fitness related services. Our training services are offered in a fully mobile arena offering mobile, corporate, gym or studio training.

The industry _____ performs services in is defined as:

Mainly Nutrition offers vitamins and agrees to exclusively recommend Achieve Fitness USA in exchange for Achieve Fitness USA exclusively recommending Mainly Nutrition.

If either party wishes to terminate this agreement the following will occur:
This agreement may be terminated at anytime by either party with (30) days notice.

Marketing: Each party may develop joint marketing campaigns as agreed upon.

Advertising: Neither party will produce any print, radio or TV advertising involving anything with the other company unless written agreement is provided by the other company which may come in the form of a standard email.

It is understood that is a mutually beneficial agreement between both our companies to refer each other on an exclusive basis to benefit both _____ and Achieve Fitness USA.

Code of Ethics: As both parties agree to be exclusively referring each other we will term our code of ethics as follows:

We will not promote any other like companies and provide referrals to any other like company as we both understand the other company is exclusively referring the other.

In case of breach of agreement: The other company may get out of this agreement without the (30) day notice.

In agreement to the exclusive arrangement;

_____   _____

Achieve Fitness USA   Vendor

_____   _____

Date   Date

Waiver of Liability

By my signature below, I affirm my participation in (your name and/or company), workouts or other program(s) of strenuous physical activity, including, but not limited to aerobic exercises, weight training, and the use of various pieces of aerobic-conditioning equipment. I further affirm that I am (at least) eighteen years of age and do not suffer from any disability that would prevent or limit my participation in this exercise program.

For myself, my heirs and assigns, I hereby release and hold harmless (your name and/or company) its employees, coaches, officers, directors, staff and/or owners, from any claims, demands and causes of action arising from my participation in this exercise program.

I fully understand that I may injure myself as a result of my participation in this exercise program, and I hereby release (your name and/or company) from any liability now or in the future. I understand the risks inherent in exercise and accept responsibility for those risks. I hold (your name and/or company) harmless for problems arising from, but not limited to, heart attacks, muscle strains, pulls or tears, broken bones, shin splints, heat prostration, knee/lower back/foot injuries and any other illness, soreness or injury, however caused, occurring during or after my participation in this exercise program.

THE UNDERSIGNED WAIVES ANY CLAIM AGAINST, RELEASES AND HOLDS HARMLESS (your name and/or company) ITS TRAINERS, COACHES OFFICERS, DIRECTORS, STAFF, AGENTS AND OWNERS FOR INJURY, INCLUDING DEATH NOT CAUSED BY WILLFUL AND WANTON ACTIONS OF ALL OF THE ABOVE PARTIES WHICH COULD FORSEEABLEY CAUSE SUCH INJURY.

I hereby affirm that I have read and fully understand the above.

_____

Print Full Name

_____

Address

_____

City, State, ZIP

_____   _____

Signature   *Date*

Medical Clearance Form

Dear Doctor _____ ,

Your patient, _____ , is interested in taking part in a fitness assessment and beginning a(n) (un)supervised exercise program. The assessment involves sub-maximal measurements of cardio-respiratory fitness, body composition, flexibility, and muscular strength and endurance. Personnel qualified in assessment techniques, CPR and first aid will administer all assessment protocols.

Your patient has completed a medical history and Physical Activity Readiness Questionnaire, which has highlighted the need for medical clearance. By completing this form, you are not assuming any responsibility for our assessment program. If, however, you know of any reason why the participant should not undertake a basic assessment of fitness, we would be most grateful if you could indicate the reason(s) below. In addition, please include any restrictions and/or limitations for your patient.

Thank you for your cooperation in this matter,
Your name and/or company name
Your company address
City, State and zipcode
Phone number

Name of patient: _____

_____ I know of no reason why the patient may not participate

_____ I recommend that the patient NOT participate.

_____ I believe the patient can participate, but I urge caution because:

_____

_____

Please be advised that my patient, _____ , should be subject to the following restrictions in the fitness assessment and/or in her exercise program:

_____

In addition, under no circumstances should she engage in the following activities:

_____

_____

Signature: _____

Address: _____

_____

Telephone: _____

SIGN UP & BILLING FORM
Credit Card & Billing Authorization Form

Client Information:

Client Name_____ Date_____

Address_____ City_____ Zip_____

Home Phone_____ Cell Phone_____

Email Address_____

Other_____

Signature_____
By signature I agree to the monthly billing plan and to its rules and regulations

By signing up for auto bill I understand that Achieve Fitness USA/Wholly Fit will not share any of the confidential information provided on this sheet with any other source. My Coach will let me know my session totals each month and will then auto bill my card. This system is put in place for the convenience of our customers. Thank you!

Please write neatly

Credit/Debit Card Information
(VISA, MASTERCARD, DISCOVER/NOVUS accepted)

NAME (as it appears on card)_____

CREDIT/DEBIT CARD TYPE_____

CREDIT CARD NUMBER_____

CARD EXPIRATION DATE_____

3-DIGIT SECURITY CODE_____

AUTO BILL_____ CC ON FILE ONLY_____ 1X CHARGE_____

All information is 100% confidential and will not be used unless authorized by the cardholder

Rules and regulations

Payments are due on the 1st or 15th day of each month. I agree as a client of Achieve Fitness USA that I will not pay my Coach individually and all payments will go thru AF-USA for services provided by this or any AF-USA representative. I understand AF-USA will bill me for an estimate if I continue working with my Coach and pay him/her directly. I agree the total due monthly will be paid to AF-USA for all personal fitness or related services that I receive from this trainer. I understand AF-USA is the agency this Coach is an employee or contractor of.

Independent Contractor New Hire Agreement/Booklet
This is an example of an agreement you can private label
to your company. In no way is this to be considered a legal
agreement provided by the authors, our representatives or
anyone associated with our company.

Achieve Fitness USA
New Hire Orientation Booklet

Dear Applicant,

Congratulations on being accepted to the Achieve Fitness USA
Team. Every new member of the AF-USA team begins the
journey to success by going through the orientation process.
It is our deepest desire to see all team members succeed and
achieve whatever personal and professional goals they have.
This orientation is the first step down the path to doing exactly
that.

This orientation booklet will cover the following topics:
- **Company Compensation Plan** - You will receive a copy of
  the company compensation plan and we will conduct a
  thorough review of the AF-USA pay structure.
- **Company Rules and Regulations Packet** - You will
  receive a copy of the company rules and regulations
  packet and a thorough review will be conducted by
  your manager.
- **Employee and/or Contractor Agreement** – Complete
  coverage and description of your formal agreement
  with the company.
- **Performance Requirements** - We will discuss and explain
  all performance requirements and expectations as
  described in your 90-day plan.
- **Company Assets and Additional Revenue Streams** –
  You will receive a complete overview and review of

the various business avenues available to company employees, contractors and partners.

- **Fundamental Fitness Products** - Learn how to leverage the relationship with our products firm, Fundamental Fitness Products, to accelerate movement toward goals.
- **Forms** - Learn how to fill-out pay form, auto credit card and billing forms, client agreements and others.
- **Mobile Fitness Training Demo and Consultation Training** – You will receive training on the Demonstration Session we perform for our equipment store partners so you can begin obtaining clients leads for mobile training. We will also provide you with a copy of our '90-days to Success' book which was written by our company president Robert Raymond and Licensing Owner Derrick Wilburn.
- **Studio Orientation System** – One (or more) of our studio manager(s) will conduct a 60 minute training and orientation on our studios and studio system process.
- **Corporate and Residential Fitness Training** - Our corporate fitness manager will conduct a 60 minute training and orientation on our corporate and residential fitness services process.

Company Review

Review of Company Business Packets and Requirements
Time: 60-90 minutes
During this first section we will review together the following
Packets page by page, answer any questions and provide you
with valuable insight as necessary.
- Compensation Plan
- Company Rules and Regulations
- Signed Agreement
- Performance Requirements
- Company goals, assets and additional revenue streams
  available to you (outline below)

Company Forms
Time: 15-30 minutes
We will instruct you on company systems for billing and our
pay forms and provide you with electronic versions of all
company forms, including:
- Billing forms (for billing clients and explanation of legal
  rights of the customer)
- Pay-day form
- Access to complete library of forms

Revenue Streams

Available revenue streams
Time: 15-30 minutes

Achieve Fitness USA offers many revenue streams. Increase opportunities for success by adding multiple revenue streams to your business. In today's fitness industry and business world it's critical to have revenue centers available to increase profits and attract quality employees and contractors.

Available Revenue Streams to AF-USA employees, contractors and Licensing Owners:

1. Mobile Fitness Training Department
2. Corporate Fitness Training Department
3. Residential Fitness Training Department
4. Profit sharing and growth programs (see compensation plan)
5. The Corporate Fitness Promotional Product Program
6. Achieve Fitness USA Lead Generator Program
7. FUNdamental FITness PROducts
8. FFP Sales Associate
9. FFP Product and Education Creation Program
10. FFP Trade Show Sales and Exhibit Schedule
11. The Therapy Zone Program
12. Fitness Camps
13. Trademarked Programming
14. Successful Venture Opportunities
15. Licensing Program Sales Opportunity

Mobile Fitness Division Training Demos and Consultation Training

Demonstration Sessions and Consultations
Time: 30-45 minute

Introduction:

Gaining new clients through our in-home training division is an excellent way to become successful quickly. Therefore, it is most important that all new trainers become properly trained on "Demonstration Sessions". Most Demo Sessions are performed through alliances with equipment stores and are a fast-track method for developing a client base in just 90 days. This section details the Consultation and Demo Session process.

History of a Demo:

The demo session was created by Robert Raymond in the early 1990s. Robert saw a great opportunity for us to develop relationships with equipment stores. By providing the store with a 'free' session, we create a unique win-win-win scenario. The free session helps the store close deals when selling equipment, it provides the customer with a quality service, and provides us with the opportunity to pick up new clients.

Success Rate:

You should a success rate of up to 8% rate on these sessions, if performed them properly.

Keeping Proper Records:

It is most important you keep an Excel spreadsheet on each and every client lead you receive even if they say 'no thanks' to your services, you are still developing a database that can be marketed to later. All prospective demos are people who are interested in fitness, those are individuals worth keeping tack of.

Long-term success is the goal:

Not all demos convert on the day of the meeting. It happens that we go out, do a demonstration sessions and at its conclusion the customer declines to hire us. Remember it is your job to be professional and show the value of working with a personal trainer. If you succeed in doing that, there's an excellent chance of working with this person in the future. We have had demos call us 2-3 years later and sign-up for services.

How long should these sessions take?

I recommend 45 minutes to an hour most.

DEMONSTRATION SESSIONS AND IN-HOME CONSULTATIONS

HINTS AND TIPS

A step-by-step description of how to:
1. **Set up the Demo**
2. **Perform the Demo/Consultation**
3. **Land a New Client**

Time: approx. 1 hour (will vary)

1. Set up the Demo

The Set up phone call:

Hello is (prospect name) available?

Hi (prospect name), this is (your name) with Achieve Fitness USA, you recently purchased a (name piece of equipment) Precor treadmill from (name of vendor), I'm calling to set up your in-home demonstration session on the piece of equipment.

After you have built a little rapport, be sure to get the following information:
1. Address (this is important- if the client is not in your area you will be able act as a liaison and be sure the trainer closest to them does the demo)
2. Phone number (ask what is the best number to contact them)
3. Age
4. Any medical or other concerns that you should be made aware of
5. Goals (Personal, Health, Fitness)
6. Exactly what piece(s) of equipment they purchased
7. What, if any, other pieces of equipment they own

Great, I am available on Tuesday or Thursday evenings between about 6 and 8, which would be an ideal time for me to come by and show you how the (equipment name) will help you achieve your goals?

<u>If the Set up call goes to an answering machine or voice mail</u>:

Remember the K.I.S.S. principle - Keep It Short and Simple. Less is more. Just leave the vital information and keep the message to a maximum of 30 seconds.

> *"Hi, (prospect name – if this is their personal voice mail) *or* (this message is for prospect name – if it is not) this is (your name) with Achieve Fitness USA. I am calling on behalf of (name of specific sales rep *if known* at [name of vendor]) to set up your complimentary demonstration session on your new (name of equipment). I will be in your area within the next week and would like to get your session scheduled today, if at all possible. Please return my call at (your phone number), again that's (repeat number). Thank you."*

Always generate some urgency by indicating you need to schedule them while you're in the area – and you'll be in the area soon! Always speak very clearly and leave your call back number twice. No one likes having to listen to a message four times in order to pick out the call back number. It's also useful to leave the number two different ways. In other words, if the number is 237-8040, the first time through say, "two, three, seven, eight, zero, four, zero". Then the second time say, "that's two, three, seven, eighty, forty." It makes things very easy to remember and eliminates confusing numbers that can sound alike, such as 256 and 266.

If you have designated times for doing demos, be sure to present those times to the prospect. It is important to have a schedule and it's much easier to get that schedule the way you would like it from the beginning - rather then trying to do once a large client base exists.

For Colorado-based trainers, once the appointment is set, call the main office 303 721 0689 leave a message stating when and with whom you have set a demo appointment. This allows us to track our demo set up and success rate, and allows us to send you other demo prospects.

2. *Perform the Demo*

If you have never done an in home demo or have never used the specific piece of equipment
being demonstrated, <u>be</u> <u>sure</u> to get into the vendor's place of business and:

1. have a sales representative give a full sales presentation on the piece(s) of equipment(s)

2. spend time becoming thoroughly familiar with the equipment's capabilities, adjustment points, strengths/ weaknesses, etc.

Be certain to schedule the demonstration session leaving enough time to complete the above steps. The last thing you want to happen is for the prospect to ask a question about the machine(s) to which you have no answer.

If you are going to demo a piece of cardio equipment, be sure and know how to program the electronics. For resistance machinery, develop a list of exercises you feel comfortable demonstrating and have a plan heading into every demo. For example, if demonstrating a Nautilus home gym, have exercises for the chest, back, shoulders, biceps, triceps, legs, and especially abdominals. Then if necessary, adapt.

Nautilus Home Gym:

Squats/Leg Press: Talk about the benefits of performing the squat and how it is relevant to every day activities. Keep it brief, one to two sentences. "Squats are important in shaping and toning the legs. It is an activity you do everyday like sitting down in a chair, or getting off the toilet." Then demonstrate how to use the attachment to set up the squat, demonstrate a proper squat.

Chest Press: Discuss the benefits and everyday applications of chest pressing, (getting out of bed, etc.). Set and explain proper seat height and shoulder alignment, then perform a proper chest press.

This pattern stays the same and repeats itself for each exercise that you go through. If the prospect has an injured body part, use that as an excellent tool for demonstrating the value of working with a fitness professional. Show how to make the most of the machine to rehab and strengthen the injured. This is a wonderful opportunity to put the prospect at ease about using the equipment and at the same time build their confidence in your abilities.

Demo Day:

1. Introduce yourself (they know who you are, after all they were expecting you)
2. First 10-20 minutes should be rapport building. Create some small talk, complement their home or location, any animals, etc. Something positive - get off on the right foot.
3. Explain or outline what you are going to do.
4. Get information on their goals. Ask "why" questions – "So why did you buy this machine?"
5. Second 20 minutes is devoted to equipment demo. Be certain to demonstration *YOUR* knowledge, more than the machine's features.
6. Last 20 minutes is for Q&A. Keep answers general and relatively vague. This is where the prospect needs to be informed this was session was simply to introduce them to their new piece of equipment. If they want something more personalized, like a program to begin following, they may be interested in a Profile and Program Design Session.
7. When approaching the 45 minute mark, act as though you have another appointment and speed things up. This is not rude! Ask if they would like to set a time to complete their Profile Session, you can explain that the information you were able to give was general. To get more specific and to get the most from their investment

you recommend a Profile Session, which includes a program designed specifically to meet the prospects goals. ALWAYS get a reason to call back

3. Land a New Client

The conclusion of the demo session is our opportunity to gain a new client. During the prior 40 minutes our skill, knowledge, personality and abilities have been on display—now, if the prospect is comfortable with us and has been properly shown the value of working with us, landing a client should be a natural next step. Landing a new client can mean one of three things:

1. Selling a Profile/Program Design Session
2. Getting a regular, recurring sessions client
3. Both

Nearly all demo sessions could and should result in a Profile Session. Practice and perfect a monolog that goes something like this, and your success rate should be very high:

> "The biggest problems we run into are people just not knowing what to do to achieve their fitness goals. Most people don't know how many repetitions are too many, or how many days a week to exercise their arms. So they attack without a plan, meaning success is a guessing game. That's not good. We provide this demonstration session as a service for (name of vendor). If you'd like to get more information on working with me personally, here you go."

Hand the prospect a business and rate card.

> "The Profile Session is where I will come back, perform an assessment on your body today, discuss goals and use that information to design a very comprehensive program for you to begin following. It takes all the guess work out of what you should be doing on a daily

and weekly basis and at just (current rate card price) is the best value we have going. I'm in this neighborhood again on Thursday, so if you'd like to get that done we can schedule it now."

Never be afraid to ask for the sale! For prospects that do not become clients, the main reason is because they are never asked.

In-Home Consultation
Time: approx. 20 minutes (will vary)

1. If a Phone Call is first contact

    a. **Introduction**

The introduction is the first thing you will say to the client. It will set the mood of the conversation. It should be precise and lead into the rest of the conversation.

"Hi, is Sandy available? Hi, Sandy, this is Darrell calling with Achieve Fitness USA. I understand you're interested in personal training. Do you have a few moments to chat?"

    b. **History**

During this stage get as much information about the client as possible. Discuss her fitness background. Determine what exercise she's doing, how often, how long and how much. Get as much information as possible on all parts of her fitness program: cardio, muscle conditioning and flexibility.

Discuss nutrition, injury status, sleeping habits and stress levels. Listen for key pieces of information. Is she a beginner? Is there an injury you can help rehabilitating? Is she neglecting key fitness components that you can address?

Ask a ton of questions. People love to talk about themselves.

If you let them you do so, they will leave the interaction thinking you are an amazing person even though you haven't told them anything about yourself. So engage your potential client in interactive conversation. Be sure to be interested in what she's saying.

c. **Goals**

Find out exactly why the client needs you. Be sure to probe so you are very clear about her expectations.

d. **Action Plan**

Here's where you get to explain how you can help. Be sure to relate everything you say back to what the client told you. Focus on the benefits she will achieve, not the features of your program. (Important note * learn the difference between features and benefits*)

e. **Conclusion**

Tie up loose ends by determining how you will work together. When and how often will you train? Book the first appointment. Determine whether you will perform a basic or comprehensive fitness assessment (Profile Session). Tell her what she can expect during the first session. Ask her to pick up, fill out and return the client questionnaire.

f. **Thank the Client!**

Note if you are arranging an appointment by phone and it is the first appointment, try to get a credit card number, this will allow you to compensated for your time and increases the chances they will value the appointment and show up.

2. If first contact is live

Same general idea and outline as above. Have an introduction in which you give a short background and summary of your qualifications. Be certain to go somewhere comfortable to talk, someplace that puts the client at ease. Neighborhood coffee shops are a good option.

Get the prospect excited by discussing goals and telling success stories of other clients you have or are working with that are seeing phenomenal results. And always try to get the prospect talking by asking leading questions, such as:

Tell me about...........................
What was that like?
Tell me how you'll look if ....
Specifically......................
Explain.....................
What specific changes are you looking for?
How would your life be better?
How often will you be exercising?
Have you discussed this with your wife/husband?

Discuss the Profile Session and end by scheduling a Profile Session.

How to Perform Consultations
A step-by-step process

This explanation is going to be simple and brief. When someone calls and is interested in hiring you the only way you can mess it up is by not being professional, not being prepared or having a bad attitude.

Steps to success

1)   Before going out to meet someone and do a consultation with them make sure to know a little bit of history on them (as in the Demo process above). Ask a few questions before going to meet with them so you show up prepared to give the answers they need.

Recommended questions
   a)   What are your goals?
   b)   Do you have any health concerns?
   c)   Do you have anything holding you back from succeeding?
   d)   Where would you like to train?

2)   Be prepared and organized when you meet and understand that, after you provide them a brief introduction, the meeting is 100% about the prospect.

3)   Be a professional. Show up dress like a fitness trainer, have excellent hygiene, and have a great motivating attitude. Remember the average client decides if they want to sign up with you in the first 14 seconds.

Understand if someone called for a consultation they want to hire you before having even met you. The only way to not get a new client is if you blow it. By being prepared and organized prior to any consultation, earning a new client is almost a certainty.

Guarantee of Results!

There is nothing wrong with using the word "guaranteed". It is one of my favorite things to do. I have always told clients I guarantee results or they get their money back. I have never had someone ask for their money back!

The 90 Success Express

Educate yourself on how to develop a client base
Time: 10 minute discussion

This book is considered one of our company bibles and it is very important to your success. We will email you a copy of this book. It is expected that you will read it immediately to begin understanding the Achieve Fitness USA system of developing a client base.

Notes:

Final

1. Brief orientation on our corporate, residential, camps and studio systems and provide the contact information to schedule the meetings with each manager from each department.
2. Answer Questions
3. Sign the completion of orientation form Below
4. Provide all contact information for questions

Notes:

Trainer Name: _____

Manager: _____

Date: _____

Appendix

Orientation Completion Form:

I acknowledge that Achieve Fitness USA has provided me the company rules and regulation packet, the compensation packet, discussed my non-compete agreement, and provided me all information provided on page 2 of this packet.

I also understand Achieve Fitness USA may update this material and I will receive all information (or) it will be posted in our offices and studios for review at anytime and is available to me.

I also understand it is my responsibility to know the compensation plan, rules and regulations guideline packet and performance obligation.

Signed_____

Date_____

Address_____

_____

Contact Phone Number_____

Email_____

The 90 Day Plan

90-day plan agreement
Anyone joining the Achieve Fitness USA team is required to develop a 90-day plan to begin with our company. This plan will consist of the following. As a new member of the Achieve Fitness USA team I agree to follow the plan set forth by my mentor who wills be

_____.

Signed_____

Date_____

The First 90 Days

Congratulations on being accepted to join the Achieve Fitness USA Team. The first 60-90 days are very important as we will now develop your business plan and goals.

To start we need to develop your short term, middle range and long-term goals.

Example: Short-term goals could be to pick up 10 hours per week training, Progressive goal #1 could be something like I want to manage something in the business, run a department, create education material etc. And your long term goal would be something like I want to take my studio system national etc. Your goals should be progressive based upon your short and long-term vision created in your interview process.
Short-Term Goals -

Progressive Goal #1

Progressive Goal #2

Implementation of your plan

Now that we have developed your (3) goal plan. How are we going to incorporate this plan on a daily basis? Please list all objectives.

1) Hours of operation and how will we implement your goals into these hours

2) Action Plan